So you want to open a yoga studio

Strategies for growing your classes,
community, and bank account

Andrew Tanner & Janis Bowersox

So You Want to Open a Yoga Studio
Strategies for growing your classes, community, and bank account

By **Andrew Tanner** and **Janis Bowersox**

Edition ISBNs

Soft cover: 978-1-938579-46-2

1st Edition, October 2012

Editors: Amy Scott and Matt Reindel
Layout: Ahreum Han-Tanner and Tudor Maier
Cover design: Ranilo Cabo

TABLE OF CONTENTS

ACKNOWLEDGMENTS

Thanks to the teachers and students in all the yoga studios we started.

Thanks to all the owners/managers we helped or who helped us, including Jen Jennings from Yoga for Everybody; Stephanie Miller, Suzanne Scholten, and Kaity Leisure from Bamboomoves; Norma Kerner from Yoganesh; and Michael Baez from Excel Yoga.

A special acknowledgment goes to Joan Dwyer and Scott Kleinfeld, two successful yoga studio owners, friends, and colleagues who ride the waves of yoga studio ownership with grace, creativity, and panache! Their stories, advice, and friendship over the years were extremely helpful in writing this book.

We would like to acknowledge Beverley Murphy, a yoga industry expert whose work has influenced thousands of business owners including us. In 2005, Beverley created MindBody University, a business intensive for MindBody Online clients. Beverley has spent the good part of a decade studying and refining the statistics she's collected from yoga studios. We attended her program and tested her recommendations in our own studios. We are also deeply appreciative of the founders of MindBody Online, CEO Rick Stollmeyer and CSMO Robert Murphy, and the rest of the folks at MBO.

Thanks to the teachers and staff at the Kripalu Center for Yoga and Health, and especially Vandita (Kate Marchesiello), for spearheading the Kripalu Yoga Teacher

Association and the Kripalu Affiliated Studios as well as championing Kripalu's Program for Diversity. Through Vandita, Kripalu has offered business support to yoga teachers all over the planet, while Kripalu Center itself continues to act as a beacon of light to those looking for health and personal growth.

Ultimately, we honor all the yoga teachers that have ever been and will be, the thread that connects us all, past, present, and future.

Namasté
Jai Bhagwan
Sat naam
Shantih

Janis's Gratitudes

To all my yoga teachers, especially:

- Susan Pataky, for introducing me to yoga

- Barbara McFerran Engel, for introducing me to Kripalu yoga

- Marleen Salko, for helping me achieve my dream (she let me run her yoga business and later sold her studio to me)

- Betsy Kase, who shared her story of how she started Yoga Haven in Tuckahoe, NY, and who taught me how to teach yoga to beginner bodies

- Carolyn Fahey (the Goddess of *Kula*), for helping me see the beauty in everyone

- Jacquie LeMeur, for modeling the change I want to see in the world

- Joy Abrams, for introducing me to mindfulness

- Kim Valeri, for bringing teacher training to my yoga studio

- Evelyne Serais, for introducing me to Kundalini yoga

To my life coach, Shantipriya (aka Marcia Goldberg), whom I met at the most vulnerable time in my life (1999). She facilitated my dream to open a yoga center.

To my mastermind group (who challenged me to write this book) and our extraordinary facilitator, Jane Pollak.

To the general manager of Yoga for Everybody, Jen Jennings; I couldn't have done it without you!

To my BFF, Barb McFerran Engel, for seeing me through all the ups and downs.

To my business advisor, Juan Scott (of Scott Associates), who helped me make critical management decisions.

To my parents, Sox and Norma Bowersox, who have always cheered me on with unconditional love.

To Ganesha, for removing the obstacles toward achieving financial independence and radiant health!

Andrew's Gratitudes

To all my yoga teachers, especially:

- Chun Shim Park, whose spiritual healing of my father opened my eyes to the world of the soul and started me on the path of yoga

- Jae Hun Lee, who taught me the world of *ki/prana* and inspired me to transform myself and work hard on my body, mind, and spirit

- Sri Dharma Mittra, who was my saving grace in dark times and who taught me the great tradition of Hatha Raja yoga

- Andrei Ram, for being a unique transmission of the divine and showing me what great yoga teachers in this modern world can strive for

- The Kripalu community of teachers and executives, whose living examples of yoga teach me on a daily basis, including Devarshi, Jovinna, David L., Hilary, Larissa, Nicole, Grace, John O., Denise, Deb, and Shobahn

To Stephen Cope, for writing *The Great Work of Your Life*, which inspired me to go for it on this book and other future projects.

To every student I have ever worked with, from Dahn to Bamboomoves, Dharma's to Kripalu, and all my private students. All of you have been my teachers as much or more than I have been yours.

To Scott Kleinfeld, Steve Wood, Sun and Tao, Daniel Flynn, Jeff Gagnon, Norma Kerner, and Joan Dwyer, for their friendship.

To my parents, Susan and Stephen Tanner, who were my first real yoga teachers because they taught me about the absolute essence of yoga, "pure love."

To my wife, Ahreum Han-Tanner, who is my pillar of strength and soul mate.

INTRODUCTION

It is better to strive in one's own dharma than to succeed in the dharma of another. Nothing is ever lost in following one's own dharma.

—Krishna in *The Bhagavad Gita*

If you are thinking about opening a yoga studio, you need to read this book! Our intention is to help you answer two very important questions: "Do I want to open a yoga studio?" and, if so, "How do I start?" We also give you advice and insights on operating a successful yoga business. Between the two of us, we have opened nine yoga studios, bought three yoga studios, and sold three yoga studios. Our businesses went from negative revenues to over $500,000 a year. We won awards, expanded, opened stores, hired full-time managers, brought in teacher training, and even licensed our own studio brands. In a word, we *succeeded*. And you can, too. Our goal is to help you get a picture of what owning a studio would be like for *you*, and to help you avoid the major pitfalls—without having to learn the hard way like we did!

There are many ways to open a studio and many types of studios to own, and this book does not cover them all. The model we are presenting is a single stand-alone studio, with space for both private and group sessions, that is open seven days a week and offers at least fifteen classes each week. It includes a community of teachers. The studio appeals to people who want to come to a variety of classes and like having flexibility in when they take class. It is a real yoga center, not just a location offering a few classes.

Our book is chock-full of best practices and helpful tidbits from our combined twenty years in the yoga industry, divided into chapters that cover everything from hiring teachers to marketing. It also includes "Om" Work sections at the end of each chapter that are designed to help you move forward with your yoga business and move one step closer to your dream. You'll also find sidebars that share our personal experiences and those of other studio owners and industry experts, as well as tips for running your own studio.

CHAPTER ONE:

Is Yoga Studio Ownership Right for Me?

Enthusiasm is one of the most powerful engines of success. When you do a thing, do it with all your might. Put your whole soul into it. Stamp it with your own personality. Be active, be energetic, be enthusiastic and faithful, and you will accomplish your object. Nothing great was ever achieved without enthusiasm.

—Ralph Waldo Emerson

So you've thought about opening a yoga studio. But have you really identified *why*? Understanding the "why" is important in all aspects of your life, especially when running a business. Before you throw yourself into the more-than-full-time job that is opening and running a yoga studio, understanding the "why" is essential. When things get tough, it's the "why" that will keep you motivated to follow through. For some, the long journey of successes and frustrations can be immensely fulfilling; for others, it can bring new stresses that negatively disrupt your yoga practice and your life. Running a yoga studio is the ultimate test of yoga off the mat. You will learn a lot. We've been there, and enjoyed the ride, and wouldn't change it for all the turmeric in India!

What kind of person are you? And, more to the point, what are you like as a businessperson? These questions are important because even if you are opening a yoga studio for all the right reasons, if you don't have the right skill set, or the right personality, you could face frustration and failure.

This chapter will start by helping you think through some questions to be sure that opening a yoga studio is right for you. The three main categories of inquiry are your motivation, your ability in business, and your health. After covering these three topics, make sure to try out the "Om" Work at the end of the chapter to gain total clarity about your "why."

Motivations: Extrinsic or Intrinsic?

The first set of questions you want to ask yourself is, "Why do I want to open a yoga studio? What motivates me?" These are big questions with no easy answers. A great place to start is by understanding the difference between extrinsic motivations and intrinsic motivations.

Extrinsic Motivations: Extrinsic motivations are drivers that have to do with material things, or are related to your external needs, like money, time off, and your work environment. If you are extrinsically motivated, you work in order to achieve a particular goal or outcome. Are you unemployed and thinking that running a yoga studio is a good career move? Are you unhappy at your current job and thinking that owning a yoga studio will allow you to regain your health and sanity? Are you looking for a way to capitalize on the current trend of yoga? Do you need to make a lot of money and have a lot of free time to be happy? Do you need your weekends off?

Intrinsic Motivations: Intrinsic motivations are internal drivers that don't depend on external pressures. If you are intrinsically motivated, you work at something for the love of that thing, and it is the work itself that fulfills you, not the result of the work. Do you feel your community desperately needs a yoga center? Does creating a sacred space for others to grow sound like your life mission? Has yoga brought you so much health, happiness, and peace that you feel you must share it with others?

Analyzing Your Answers: If you answered each question about intrinsic motivation with an emphatic "Yes," then it is likely that opening a yoga studio—with a smart business plan, the right team, and a great coach—will bring you great joy and fulfillment. However, a "Yes" to any of the questions about extrinsic motivation is a red flag. This doesn't mean you shouldn't open a yoga studio; it just means you need to prepare yourself very well before opening a yoga studio, and consider that this may not be the right path for you. Though owning a yoga studio can be lucrative and you can eventually set yourself up with a comfortable schedule, it is almost always a challenging road.

While you think about whether you have the right motivations to sustain you on your journey, you must also think about *what you want*. This is much the same question, but with a different focus, for even if you have the drive to sustain you, you need to make sure that you want the job you will be creating for yourself.

This is particularly important for yoga teachers. You love yoga; that's a given. Do you want to create a community, a *sangha*, a *kula*? Or would you rather just teach? Some amazing yoga teachers with drive, passion, and charisma have opened their own studios only to find that the business side of things is too overwhelming. So you need to ask yourself if there is an existing studio that you'd rather be a part of, without being the owner. Or do you have a burning desire to create something new?

If teaching is your main goal, there are three paths that will likely be more fulfilling than opening a yoga studio on your own: renting a space for your practice, teaching at someone else's studio, or finding a business partner. Many teachers who have opened studios would have made the same amount of money, worked fewer hours, and perhaps have been more fulfilled, if they had rented space—at a church, for example—or taught at someone else's studio. They would have gotten all the joy of community and teaching without having to worry about marketing or hiring and firing employees. If you do want to create a special space in your community, but know you will need help with the business side, then perhaps seeking out a partner with business skills and a shared vision is the way to go.

Mind-Set of a Business Owner

When you open a business, you will face a number of new and different challenges. In this section, we will look at some of the demands of a business—demands that you will need to meet, either on your own or with the help of someone you work with. Make sure you feel comfortable with each question posed below.

Realistic Expectations: First off, because it's worth repeating: is your primary motivation to make lots of money? If making six figures is important to you, know that you have a long road ahead. You *can* earn a living as a yoga studio owner, but it takes time, and a lot of effort, and there are no guarantees that your studio will be successful.

Being Business-Like: Are you business - and tech-savvy? If you think you can just pray to Ganesha and be successful...good luck! Embracing the business side of running your studio will go a long way toward success. Do you work well on computers? Have you ever managed a budget (do you manage your personal finances)? If you currently don't keep track of your personal finances in a clear spreadsheet and don't have set goals for spending and saving, then this would be a great place to start before being responsible for a business. If you've run a business before, or run your own life like a business, you've got a head start. As you find good employees or a business partner, you can split the workload and focus on the parts of the business that inspire you.

> **Expected Earnings**
>
> A successful studio owner can expect to earn about $50–75K a year by his or her third year in operation. At Bamboomoves, Andrew's first studio in Queens, New York, he and his partner were able to earn this amount in their first year. This was accomplished by working six days a week, teaching many classes and manning the desk themselves.

Committed to Growth: Are you committed to life-long learning? To have a successful yoga center, you need to be inspired so you can inspire others. Your practice of yoga needs to deepen, to grow and evolve. Finding the ways, time, and money to rejuvenate yourself through training and experiences will invigorate your practice and feed your soul. You should build time and money into your business plan for your own self-care. Your studio needs to grow and change in order to attract and retain students. This means learning about the business side of owning a studio as well. Even if you find someone to manage the budget or to handle the marketing of your studio, you will still want to keep track of that information and learn to understand it.

Resourceful and Handy: Have you ever unclogged a toilet, painted a room, or used spackle or sheetrock? If so, great! If not, you will want to find someone who can help with problems that arise, and on short notice. Choosing a good space for your studio to begin with will make life easier, but you will still have to deal with lots of pragmatic issues such as heating and cooling your studio and handling repairs or computer breakdowns. Will you be ready to respond to whatever challenges your studio throws your way?

Persona of Service: Can you stay positive? You will need to be positive about your business, and radiate that positivity even when it's not quite true or you are having a tough day. This is what we call having a persona of service. Students will come to your studio to get away from the stresses of the world, so you need to keep the stresses of running a business away from your students. You can be vulnerable, but you cannot complain to your students or they will feel guilty and not enjoy being at your studio. Again, we stress the importance of building time into your business plan for self-care, meditation, yoga, and healing. If you're like Tigger, who sees the glass half full even when it's almost empty, you've got the personality of a leader who will inspire her employees and students. But as a studio owner, your ability to set an intention and stick with it through thick and thin will be tested to the fullest. Staying positive through it all is crucial.

Be in Good Health

Being in the yoga business, there is absolutely no excuse to let your health go. In order to inspire your students, you should be an example of the benefits of yoga. That doesn't mean you need to be able to put your foot behind your head or do fifty *chatterangas*, but it does mean you need to be healthy, balanced, and happy. It takes energy and vitality to run a yoga studio. For the first year you could be putting in sixty-to-eighty-hour work weeks (unless you have the resources to hire and train full-time managerial staff from the beginning). If you are currently burned out from a job that you hate, or you are in a poor state of health, you need to take time to detox and heal before starting a venture like opening a yoga center. You need to be at your best.

Your Body Never Lies

Janis learned the hard way that studio ownership can be taxing physically. At first she enjoyed the long hours and hard work. Later, she began to have aches and pains and was diagnosed with polymyalgia and rheumatoid arthritis. How much of this was related to stress? Janis is willing to bet most of it was. It took a few years of excellent self-care, including eliminating inflammatory foods like gluten as well as balancing out her hormones (naturally), combined with tai chi and the excellent teachings of Jon Kabat Zinn's program in Mindfulness-Based Stress Reduction, but she is now pain-free and drug-free and enjoys radiant health. Hiring an excellent general manager for her studio made a big difference, too.

Conclusion

Studio ownership will be a challenging but wonderful experience for you—and you will likely be successful—if you:

- can be both an owner and a yoga teacher;
- are physically and mentally fit with abundant energy;
- love yoga and are committed to life-long learning;
- are business- and tech-savvy; and
- have a persona of service.

"Om" Work

Go out to tea with a friend (or have a Skype chat with tea in hand) and have your friend ask you all of the questions we have raised here in this chapter. Ask your friend to listen to your answers and repeat back what they hear you saying for each answer. As you listen to them repeat back your answers, notice what comes up for you. After the conversation, write a journal entry that answers the question "Why do you want to open a yoga studio?"

CHAPTER TWO

What Does Your Dream Studio Look Like?
Vision, Mission, Identity

Whatever you do, or dream you can, begin it. Boldness has genius and power and magic in it.

—Goethe

You need to have conviction to open a studio and see it through the challenges that will certainly arise. But more importantly, any good business needs to have a clear vision for the future, a mission to take you there, core values that define your identity, and a brand that embodies who you are—while also speaking to the public's needs. This chapter will provide you with some questions and examples on how to begin formulating your vision, mission, and identity. We will discuss your "brand" in the chapter on marketing.

Understanding Your Vision and Mission

A **vision** describes the ultimate goal of your business, what will happen if you do your mission well. A vision is your raison d'être, your reason for being. It should be future sighted, and the thought of accomplishing it should send chills down your spine. Your vision needs to motivate you, inspire your commitment and that of others, and generate energy in your community. The vision should also be somewhat of a stretch or challenge for you so that it pushes you to strive for excellence. At the same time, the vision must be one in which you believe strongly enough that you can convince others to join you in achieving it. Lastly, a good vision is simple and clear enough to be remembered and explained easily.

A **mission** describes exactly how you are going to achieve your vision. Your mission may shift and change over time to fully achieve your vision, but it is what you live by; it must be what you strive to do best every day. In order to come up with a mission statement, you will want to consider your unique competencies and values and how that aligns with what the world needs. In other words, you will have to know your **identity** (we'll get to that in a minute).

Here are examples of company vision/mission statements from several yoga studios and major corporations. Notice that YoGanesh and All That Matters combine their vision and mission into one statement, while Google and Amazon define their statements as either a vision or a mission. For Kripalu Center you can see their vision *and* mission:

- **YoGanesh Yoga:** To create a compassionate and loving environment for the practice of various traditions of Yoga, and to achieve optimal wellness, healthy body, mind, and spirit.

- **All That Matters:** To work together with a group of talented people to educate and support each other and our community to continually grow and maintain optimal health and well-being.

- **Google:** Google's mission is to organize the world's

information and make it universally accessible and useful.

- **Amazon:** Our vision is to be earth's most customer-centric company; to build a place where people can come to find and discover anything they might want to buy online.

- **Kripalu Center:** Kripalu's vision is to build an awakened, compassionate, and connected world. Kripalu's mission is to empower people and communities to realize their full potential through the transformative wisdom and practice of yoga.

Three Parts to Your Studio's Identity

After you've honed in on your vision and mission, you can start to create an identity for your new studio. Your **studio's identity** will be a combination of three factors: the size and scope of what your studio offers, the lineage or style it comes from, and the people who go there (your target market or ideal clients).

A Personal Vision

Some people prefer to make a personal vision before making a vision for their business. When Andrew was starting out as a yoga teacher, his vision was "To be a warrior of peace that helps heal the world." The vision for the first yoga studio he managed was "To bring health, happiness, and peace to the individual, the community, and the world." That vision was a perfect match for him, and he worked with great enthusiasm. Another example of a personal vision is that of Swami Kripalu, inspiration for Kripalu Center for Yoga and Health, who said, "I am a pilgrim on the path of love." Swami Kripalu's vision of himself has become a mantra for action for thousands of Kripalu teachers over the years.

Size and Scope of Your Studio:

- **Class-based only:** This sort of identity focuses solely on classes and workshops as the main mission and source of income. This sort of studio can be a one-room studio with a small desk (and a home office if there's no room at the studio) and only one or a few teachers. In its simplest form, a class-based studio can be held in smaller spaces or even out of the home. This sort of studio works great in a community that does not have much awareness of yoga and could in the future grow into a holistic learning center. This is also a great option for teacher-owners who wish to have more free time and run a simplified business. This type of studio is a viable business model all by itself.

- **Holistic learning center:** This sort of identity will bring in more than just yoga classes to your business. You will also be concerned with fostering community and holistic health awareness through workshops and healing services. This sort of vision will require a larger amount of space, multiple rooms, stronger organizational and business skills, and likely more investment than a class-based business. Bringing in more than just classes allows for multiple streams of income and a larger variety of services for your community. Extra classroom space makes it easy to offer immersion workshops like teacher training. Also, if you offer teacher trainings, you will have plenty of space for new teachers to test their chops. This sort of studio works great in a metropolitan area or a suburban area with a wealthy/educated population. Bringing this sort of offering to less affluent communities will be addressed in Chapter 3: Finding the Right Space.

Lineage/Style:

- **Eclectic/multiple styles of yoga and movement:** Will you welcome various styles and philosophies of yoga into your school? (Hatha, Vinyasa, Gentle, Restorative, Ashtanga, Tai-Chi, Zumba, etc.) This is an open-minded approach that works well for community-center spaces. This will allow your studio to appeal to a variety of people. This style probably makes sense for most owners, unless they have been taught and immersed in a particular lineage, or have a strong group of teachers who all share a single style. One disadvantage of this system is that your community and teachers may at times be at odds with each other; for example, an alignment-based Iyengar teacher may be telling students to do postures differently than a vinyasa flow–based teacher. It's important that the studio owner sets the tone for teachers to accept each other's differences and allow students to make their own choices about what works for them.

- **Style-based:** The style-based approach (Iyengar, Kripalu, Kundalini, etc.) can limit your studio, but it can also streamline and simplify how you run your business. Workshops, teacher trainings, and classes will not share conflicting messages, and will be set up to guide students into deepening a specific practice. The community you develop will be strong and students will benefit from becoming part of the lineage. This type of studio is much more likely to succeed in an area with a high population density. In a major city where the pool of possible yoga students is large, a focus on a particular lineage could help distinguish your studio from other studios. One disadvantage to having a lineage- or style-based studio is that any scandal in the lineage could hurt your studio's good name. However, the biggest factor in determining whether to offer multiple styles of yoga or to focus on a single style should always be your vision for the studio and what you are passionate about. We only recommended a style-based studio if you are deeply established in and committed to a particular lineage.

- **Brief thoughts on hot yoga:** Currently, hot yoga is very popular as a health craze, and many find it to be a spiritually uplifting detoxifying practice. We do not have experience running a hot yoga studio, but we do feel it limits your ability to run other types of programming. Other drawbacks are that you will be working in a stinky, sweaty sauna seven days a week! Admittedly, there are many successful entrepreneurs running hot yoga studios, and we recommend you reach out to any of them if hot yoga is your passion.

Your Target Market/Ideal Clients:

- **Young and athletic students/working professionals:** Members of Gen X and Gen Y are often drawn to challenging classes like Bikram or vinyasa and are more likely to attend classes in the early morning, after work, and on weekends. The demographic in general is perhaps initially less interested in the spiritual aspects of yoga and more interested in the physical benefits; however, they are usually open-minded enough to try spiritual workshops offered. They would seek classes that make them sweat and move. A mix of popular and spiritual music will affect Gen X and Gen Yers positively because they have grown up with MTV and ear buds in their ears most of the time. They may be uncomfortable in a silent or gentle class. While members of this group may not initially be spiritually focused, their youthful passion makes them the most likely group to eventually take teacher training or immersion programs.

- **Middle-aged and baby boomer students:** Most people in this group will want weekends, late-afternoon, and evening classes. Some parents, professionals with flexible schedules, and people who don't work (like the very rich and unemployed) will enjoy morning classes. Offerings may be more along the levels of gentle, mixed, and restorative-type classes, with far fewer classes at a higher difficulty. Your schedule will have a mix of classes to meet people at their level, so you will need to offer more classes of each type in order to satisfy the needs of each sub-market.

- **Family-oriented center:** This demographic is younger than the baby boomers and is establishing or balancing career and family. Your studio would need to offer prenatal, kids, and family classes, and perhaps babysitting as well. Classes tend to be mixed-level and vinyasa style.

> **Hot Mamas**
>
> Don't schedule a prenatal class after a sweaty power vinyasa class. The pregnant women are already hot enough and will not be happy spending an hour in a hot room.

Your studio will likely incorporate a unique mix of scope, style, and clients. As important as it is to visualize these things as you begin to plan your studio, it is also important to understand that you will need to adapt to different circumstances. You might offer a restorative class with

Janis's Vision

In 1999, Janis took a workshop on "Exploring Your Life's Mission" during her first visit to the Kripalu Center for Yoga and Health. She identified her vision as "Using my energy to help others." Given her unique background in property management and business, and her love of yoga, she felt that opening a yoga center in her community would be fulfilling, profitable, and in line with her life purpose.

a great teacher, only to find over a few months that it's not attracting enough students to be financially viable, or you might be unable to offer a class that you envisioned because you don't have a teacher who can teach in that style. Your studio will ultimately be a compromise between what you envision and what your circumstances allow.

Conclusion

Your mission and vision will inform the choice of your studio's ideal identity. Your students' needs and desires will also affect your studio's identity, as will the look, location, and feel of your space. Chapter 3 is all about finding a location that will attract the type of students who will resonate with your mission and vision, and setting the space up for success.

"Om" Work

Now that you are familiar with what we mean by vision, mission, and identity, spend a few days creating a vision board and reflecting and journaling on the following questions and then begin to put to paper your vision, mission, and identity:

Vision: What changes do I want to see in myself? My community? The world? What would things look like if those changes were achieved? Does this vision truly make me happy? Does this vision need a yoga studio in it?

Mission: What do I need to do to achieve my mission? What are my unique competencies? What are the specific gifts I want to share with the world?

Identity: Start a "vision board." Look for pictures, words, quotes, and colors that you love in magazines or online. Cut out, print out, or draw yourself anything that you are drawn to, and tack it onto a large bulletin board or paste it on a piece of poster board. Watch as your studio identity unfolds before your eyes. Ask yourself: What would your future yoga studio look like? What are the colors? Feel like? How big is it? How many people are you imagining inside it? Who are those people? What are you doing in the studio? How are people acting there?

CHAPTER THREE

Finding the Right Space

Don't open a shop unless you like to smile.

—Chinese Proverb

Now that you've mapped out your vision and mission and begun to think about your studio's identity, you will quickly come to realize that nothing sets the tone for your studio more than the location and physical space itself. In other words: It's all about the space. You are going to offer inspiring classes with excellent teachers, and cultivate the community that your students long for, and the studio space is the vessel you create to manifest these goals. We have identified six key factors that you will need to take into consideration for finding and obtaining your space:

1. Size and shape of the primary yoga room
2. Beyond the classroom
3. Location
4. Existing interior quality
5. Landlord relationship
6. The lease

1. Size and Shape of the Primary Yoga Room

For starters, you'll need space to comfortably hold at least twenty, and preferably more than twenty-five, students in a class. If your space is any smaller, you'll end up paying your teachers and your rent, but not yourself. The only type of studio owners that can get away with a smaller space are the ones who plan to teach all the classes, because they can at least pay themselves as the teacher. Otherwise the numbers just won't add up. (We will cover how you actually make money in *Chapter 6, Turning Streams of Income into a Waterfall.*) Ideally, you'll have a minimum of 750 square feet—1,000 square feet would be even better—in your main yoga room. Though you may not fill the classroom every day, having a big space makes it easier to rent it out for events and draw big-name yoga teachers who can fill the house for workshops.

The range of space needed per student varies greatly depending on the style of yoga. For a vinyasa class, a student will likely only take up the space on their mat, which is generally 12–14 square feet (six or seven feet by two feet), plus some space around them, so the minimum space we recommend is about eighteen square feet. This leaves about one foot between mats laterally and vertically. This may feel like a tight squeeze for some, but it will help you calculate the maximum number of people you can reasonably fit in your studio. For a restorative or prenatal class, thirty-two square feet per student lets each student really spread out and gives enough space for the teacher to give delicious assists. With a 1,000-square-foot studio, you can still fit close to thirty students in this spread-out way. Don't forget that the teacher also needs a place to teach from. We recommend imagining that the teacher takes up forty square feet, a little more than two mat spaces.

The shape of the room is just as important as the total floor space. A long, super-thin rectangle will limit your classroom setup, and an L-shaped or funky-shaped room won't serve you as well, no matter what the square footage. We recommend a 1,000-square-foot room that measures 25' x 40' as the ideal ratio. If you find the perfect location but the main room is not the right size, you could renovate and move walls to create the ideal space. Square spaces are also OK, unless you teach in a style that depends on using the walls, in which case you will have a lot of dead space in the center of the room. Any space less than twenty feet wide will be very uncomfortable to teach in. Space for cubbies, blocks, rental mats, straps, bolsters, and blankets is typically laid out across the back wall of the studio.

Super Cool Studio Tool

When you are looking at studio spaces, bring a tape measure, or, better yet, get a laser-pointer distance measurer, available at Home Depot or your local hardware store for around $20. (It will save you a lot of walking, getting up on chairs, asking someone to hold the tape, etc.—and you will feel really cool, too!) With this device, within one minute you can measure the square footage and ceiling height of a space.

The number of students you can fit in a room also depends on your clients—older clients living in suburbs will demand more space than young city folk. The yoga business is seasonal, so you'll need a room that can hold your overflowing crowd during the busiest time of the year (mid-January). You'll want to take all this into account when you start projecting your revenue and class sizes, so you will be able to fit enough people in the room comfortably to make your business viable.

2. Beyond the Classroom

Besides a main classroom, you will need:

- A lobby or front desk area
- A bathroom
- Changing rooms or spaces
- Closet/storage space
- An office/private space
- A second classroom or private room (optional)

Lobby: This is a place for students to sign in. It is also a place to congregate and connect, hang coats and store shoes, post flyers, get a drink of water, and check the lost and found. If you don't have a separate lobby, you can use some sort of tall structure (like bookcases) to separate out the main classroom from the lobby; but be aware that this setup makes it difficult for anyone working at the front desk to talk to clients while class is going on. Ideally, you will have enough space for people to enjoy being in your studio, a few places for people to sit down to put on their shoes, and a wall of retail items pertinent to your studio's offerings. The more people hang around your studio, the more connected they will feel, and the more likely they are to read or inquire about workshops, special offers, and retail items. (150–500 sq. ft.)

Bathroom: You need a bathroom, preferably two, located outside the yoga room and in such a way that one does not have to walk through the classroom to get to the bathroom. If you plan to install a bathroom, check where the plumbing piping is located and note where you want your bathroom to be. If the plumbing isn't in a good location, it will be *very* expensive to run the pipes from one end of the rental space to the other, and you will likely need building permits, which are costly, time consuming, and open the building up to more scrutiny. Sometimes this becomes a deal-breaker when looking for a space. Showers are also costly (and overrated unless you have a hot-yoga studio or power-vinyasa studio). The square footage for new toilets and showers will depend on your ADA laws. It's best to use the existing facilities, even if they are a bit dated, to avoid dealing with costly permits and scrutiny. (50–300 sq. ft.)

Changing Rooms: Changing rooms are a plus (especially if you have clients who come before or after work), but not a requirement. They can be separated by men and women or, if cubbies are outside the changing rooms, they can be small single-person stalls. In some studios, makeshift changing rooms can be created with shoji screens or curtains. (50–100 sq. ft. total, 25 sq. ft. per space)

Closets and Storage Space: This space can sometimes be combined with the changing rooms. If you have high ceilings, you can put some shelves about seven feet up, out of people's way.

Office Space: Having separate office space is more important than many people realize. The office space is often used as a space for you to have private conversations with students or teachers, which is valuable when difficult conversations come up around finances or etiquette. You will also want a secure room to hold cash and inventory. (100–200 sq. ft.)

Second Classroom or Private Room: An optional second classroom or private room can be used for small classes and private yoga sessions, or rented out to someone who offers complementary services, such as a massage therapist or acupuncturist. Certain types of tenants may affect your insurance costs, but partnering with a talented

Laying Pipe

In Andrew's first Bamboomoves studio, it would have cost another $7,000 to lay pipe from where the bathroom was to the front of the building, so instead they kept the bathroom behind the yoga room. This was a big mistake he never made again! Students had to do a "walk of shame" through a full classroom to use the bathroom, which disturbed the class and garnered many complaints! Though we recommend looking for a space where you don't need to change the location of the bathrooms, if everything else is perfect then the investment could be worth it.

What Goes Up May Come Down

Before Yoga for Everybody opened, Janis's significant other put up a wall to create an office, two changing rooms, and a lobby. Five years later, the wall came down, increasing the size of the classroom by 50%, and the changing rooms and lobby were moved to a new space across the hall.

acupuncturist, naturopath, or chiropractor is a creative way to bring additional students into your studio and a great service to offer your community. Your studio will be perceived as a one-stop shop for health!

Remember this: Nothing stays the same! We've put up walls, knocked them down, created offices, and expanded into neighboring space. Imagine different ways your studio space might evolve over time.

3. Location

Zoning: Before you get too excited about any space, make sure it's zoned for use for yoga. In some towns or cities any commercial zoning will be allowed, but in other places you may need to be zoned a physical cultural establishment. Check with your local building department about the zoning laws in your area.

Demographics: Maybe you already know where you want to open your studio, but the very first thing you should do is check out the demographics of the area. You can do this via Wikipedia, but it's best if you are also personally familiar with the neighborhood and are aware of the types of people in the community and how a yoga studio will be received by them. Studies have shown that people typically like to shop or hang out in areas that are equal to or slightly above their actual socioeconomic level (which is why people spend $4 on coffee at Starbucks). Therefore, to attract the most students, you will want to open in an upper-middle-class community, because people from less-affluent communities are more likely to drive a reasonable distance to practice at your space. If your goal is to bring yoga to a lower socioeconomic demographic, then we strongly recommend that you partner with an existing successful community center in that neighborhood, such as a church or YMCA. Or, you can offer free classes throughout that community. However, because of the current industry trends, we simply cannot recommend opening a brick and mortar studio in a lower-socioeconomic community. We hope to one day be able to revise this paragraph, and we are encouraged by the recent movement within the yoga community to bring yoga to more underserved populations.

Signage: Ideally, your space has existing signage that is

Underserved Populations

For two examples of inspiring associations working to bring yoga to underserved populations, check out the Yoga for All Cooperative in Connecticut (a nonprofit arm of Yoga for Everybody started by Jacquie LeMeur with the support of the current owner, Evelyne Serais, http://www.yogaforallco-op.org) and the Teaching for Diversity Program at the Kripalu Center for Yoga and Health (http://www.kripalu.org/be_a_part_of_kyta/137/).

viewable from the street by drivers and pedestrians. It is much easier and less expensive to change an existing sign than it is to apply for permits to install a new one.

Second Floor or Higher: Not being at street level is usually cheaper and quieter. Very few first-floor spaces are worth the price unless you are a retail guru. Even better would be to move in above a complementary business.

Complementary Businesses: Look for complementary businesses such as coffee shops, health food stores, etc. and locate near them. Also think about the quality of those shops compared to your brand. If your ideal student is going to Starbucks three times a week, be within one block of Starbucks!

Beware Smelly and Noisy Neighbors: Watch out for spaces located near restaurants and dance studios and other smelly or noisy places. If a space you are considering is above a restaurant, it is very important that you visit that space on a Friday night when there is a lot of cooking going on and see how well the smell is ventilated. Stinky fried-food smells can be a major turnoff when your students are in *shavasana*! Also beware of tenants to the sides or below the space who might object to jumping and music, if you plan to have any.

Drive-By and Foot Traffic: Having drive-by and foot traffic will increase awareness—a location close to or in the center of town is great, because it makes your studio part of the community and a "place to be."

Parking: Parking is a big plus but not a deal-breaker in most areas. Whether there is street parking or a parking lot, you need to be able to park 10–20 cars within a block or two (unless it's a city with great public transport, like

NYC, then forget the parking!). Also remember that if your studio is on a street that only allows one-hour street parking, your students aren't going to be able to take a class. Leaving class to find a ticket on their car will make people not want to come back, no matter how good the class.

Locations to Avoid: Strip malls lack windows and character. STAY AWAY! Also avoid locations that are off the beaten path— they are hard to find and unwelcoming.

> **One Studio's Parking Story**
>
> At Yoga for Everybody in Fairfield, CT, the only available parking was two-hour street parking. To build goodwill with her students and staff and take away some of the anxiety of keeping a watch on the clock, Janis offered to pay for their first parking ticket. It took Janis two years to successfully petition the town to increase the parking time to three hours on her street! It was a motivating and sangha-building experience.

4. Existing Interior Quality

Windows and Ceilings: We *love* windows; enough to bring in natural light, but not too many or too low. You will also need enough windowless wall space for students to do handstands or put their legs up against the wall. The ceiling should be at least eight feet high, and could be up to twelve feet (think about a six-foot-nine student being able to stretch up high without hitting ceiling fans or the ceiling). Note: a building with eighteen-foot ceilings can look enticing, but just think of the heating bills.

Flooring: Hardwood and attractive laminate are great choices. Bamboo and cork are also environmentally friendly options that are quite affordable. Of course the most environmentally friendly floor is the one that the last tenants left you! We definitely recommend not using carpets due to the smells and need for upkeep. Make sure if you are installing your own flooring that the sub-floor does not have any moisture issues; this will cause huge problems down the road and will ruin laminate flooring. Also, if the tenant below you is a loud restaurant, know that there are materials which can be installed in your sub-floor to block out the sound. At one of Andrew's studios in NYC, the restaurant downstairs was willing to pay for $10,000 of sound baffling material to be put in the floors!

Quality of the Heating/AC: Who is responsible for the heating and AC? How well does it work? Is it adequate to handle your needs? Can you control the thermostat? Is the system quiet? If the pipes start banging when the heat comes on, your student's *shavasana* and meditation practices will be compromised. HVAC systems are expensive to replace and there is nothing worse than a freezing classroom in February or a sweat lodge in July. Despite the expense, if there is one element of the studio besides decor that we recommend investing in, it would be an excellent HVAC system. Some landlords who are desperate for new tenants will install a brand-new system, so don't be afraid to ask and to use this as a negotiation point while discussing the lease terms. HVAC systems can run between $5,000 and $20,000 depending on the size and location of the installation.

Interior Design: There are many other books and resources on this subject, so we won't go into much detail. When you're looking for a space, don't worry about what the interior design looks like. You will create this from scratch once you get the right layout. Remember that the above-mentioned key points are the most costly to change, so focus on those.

5. Landlord Relationship

Will your relationship with your landlord be trying or supportive? Will he or she be a thorn in your side or a cheerleader? In our experience, a typical landlord doesn't care about your business; he or she just wants to get paid on time. He prefers little to no complaints, wants your respect, and hopes that your business will have a minimal amount of wear and tear on his building. He won't want to get involved with parking and building problems or spend money on heating, roofing, or anything! So pick your landlord carefully. The state of the real estate rental market will determine how hungry your landlord is for a tenant, or how desperate you are for a space.

> **Your Landlord Also Picks You!**
>
> In Janis's case, it took a year for her landlord to agree to rent her the space. He didn't like the idea of a lot of foot traffic in his building. He finally said yes to a personal letter. The space was ideal, but Janis went through hell and back again over issues with him. The furnace broke one February and wasn't replaced until October!

Let your landlord know what kind of a business you are opening. You will be operating seven days a week from early in the morning until late at night. When there is a building problem, like no heat or no water, you can't wait a few days for it to get fixed! It's a telltale sign of trouble if your landlord isn't willing to give you an emergency contact number that someone will answer and respond to from 6 a.m. until 10 p.m. seven days a week.

Talk to your landlord about your expectations for each other and build these into your lease. If your expectations for how the other will act don't match up, it's much better to find out up front, rather than a year later in the middle of a crisis. As a fellow entrepreneur once told us, "The devil you know is better than the devil you don't know." Landlord angels are few and far between; most are reasonable people who are a victim of the very nature of the landlord / tenant relationship.

6. The Lease

Our best advice for negotiating a lease is to hire or befriend a competent lawyer who you can trust and who is familiar with commercial real estate law. Second, do some online research to educate yourself on the components of a lease. Finally, never allow yourself to be pressured into signing a lease too quickly that you don't fully understand. Besides these three main points, there are also a few additional considerations.

Good Guy Guarantee: Sign the lease as an LLC only, to protect yourself legally. Your landlord will prefer that you sign as an individual, or sign what's called a "personal guarantee," which is essentially the same as signing as an individual. In a tough economy you can negotiate and say you are not willing to sign a personal guarantee, but if you really want the space, a great compromise is known as the "good guy guarantee." With a good guy guarantee or good guy clause you are taking personal responsibility for the lease; however, you are given a way out of the lease in case you want to break the lease early. For example, if you sign a ten-year lease and after two years your business is bankrupt and you want to throw in the towel, a typical good guy clause will allow you to break the lease by forfeiting your security deposit and giving the landlord anywhere from one to three months of additional rent. Often this additional rent can be paid in installments, and it is certainly better than being legally liable for the eight years left on the lease!

Work To Be Done Before Moving In: Check every square foot of your space before you sign the lease and use any problems that you find as bargaining chips with the landlord. Do the windows open and close, and do they have screens? Does the door hardware work smoothly? How about toilets and sinks? Are you putting in a new floor or adding a bathroom? In many cases, landlords are willing to do a lot of construction for you in order to lock you into a lease. Negotiate whatever you can. Keep in mind, however, that the landlord might not do the work the way you want it done! You need to be very specific if your landlord is doing any construction for you. Make sure you agree to all the details before signing anything. An example would be putting in a floor or a bathroom; make sure you approve of the tiles, fixtures, or flooring types to be used before signing the lease.

Noisy or Smelly Neighbors: Sometimes when you move in the neighbors aren't noisy or smelly, but you want to make sure things stay that way. Most leases require that the landlord provide you with "quiet enjoyment" of your space. You should also add a clause that protects you from "disturbing odors." This way if a new neighbor moves in, it will be the landlord's responsibility to make sure their sounds or smells do not disturb you.

Clarify Who Will Handle Emergencies: You want to make sure that your landlord will take responsibility for all basic issues like roof leaks, HVAC repairs, security systems, and plumbing and electrical issues. In case anything happens that needs emergency repair, you should be given the name and number of the building manager or super, or, if your building doesn't have one, you should have a written agreement that you can fix the problem yourself and deduct the cost from your rent.

Parking: See if you can get some designated spaces, or make sure that none are designated, so your students have plenty of options. We've seen parking become a major issue of contempt between neighboring tenants.

Permission To Sublet or Assign: This is an important clause to request. You want to make sure that you can rent out portions of your studio without any recourse and also be able to sell your studio or assign your lease to another tenant if you wish to get out of the lease.

Conclusion

Take the time to find the right space. Hold out for your ideal location if you can—there are plenty of other things you can do in the meantime. If you are willing to work hard and perform construction, you'll be able to transform an adequate space into something special!

To recap, here is our yoga space wish list:

- At least 750 sq. ft. of space—preferably 1,000—for the yoga room
- Enough windows to let in natural light
- Lots of wall space
- High ceilings, 10–12 feet
- Flooring that is structurally sound and attractive
- Quality, functional heating and AC
- Second floor or higher (quieter, often cheaper)
- High-traffic area but quiet (visibility)
- Complementary businesses (coffee shops, health food stores, etc.)
- Parking (street parking for longer than an hour)

- No smelly (restaurants) or noisy (dance studios) neighbors
- A second, smaller room (small classes, private sessions)
- Bathrooms (preferably two, and separate from the yoga room)
- Changing rooms
- Lobby space and an office / sign-in room
- A supportive landlord (who loves yoga!)
- A 3–5 year lease (signed as an LLC, not an individual) with an option to renew at the same rent for an additional 5–7 years and a "good guy guarantee"
- Well-defined roles for tenant and landlord around who is responsible for what (repairs, emergencies)
- An emergency phone number from the landlord

"Om" Work

Spend a week walking the streets of your ideal neighborhood with your eyes looking at first- and second-floor spaces for rent. Bring a pad of paper and jot down numbers and addresses. Later, make at least five phone calls to inquire about the rent being asked for each space to get an idea of what prices are like.

CHAPTER FOUR

Marketing on a Budget

There is no scarcity of opportunity to make a living at what you love; there's only a scarcity of resolve to make it happen.

—Wayne Dyer

You've developed your mission and your vision of your dream yoga studio, and your studio's identity, including what your yoga style is, who your ideal customers are, and what you're offering. While you are looking for the perfect space you will also want to begin preparing your marketing plan. We have four simple rules when it comes to marketing:

1. You MUST do it!

2. Have a distinctive brand

3. Make an irresistible offer and follow-up

4. Your brand and offer need multiple platforms to sit on

Marketing Rule #1: You MUST Do It!

Many new business owners, no matter what field they're in, believe that having a good product or service and bringing it to market is all it takes to be successful. This is a pipe dream! Marketing is the ongoing effort that all yoga studios (and businesses) need to make to be successful—and if you excel at it, your studio will also thrive. So let's be clear: marketing is not optional. Repeat after us: "Marketing is NOT OPTIONAL!" If you don't enjoy it, hire someone who does. You or a business partner will still need to oversee these efforts. Your marketing strategy is a key component in attracting the kinds of students that create the vibe you are envisioning for your studio. Attracting and retaining students in a way that fills your program and your bank account is key to your studio's viability and vitality.

To ensure that you actually do marketing, it's a great idea to create a marketing calendar.

- Plan out your year-long marketing campaigns. Be creative with the seasons and holidays.

- Anticipate the slow season (summer). Offer a summer special. Offer classes on the beach or in a park.

- Create gift certificates and special packages for December and February, which can also be slow times for class participation.

To have a well-run, effective marketing plan, you'll need to love marketing or hire help. You can hire an office manager who handles all the marketing. You can hire an outside consultant to help with any or all of it. You can find other business owners to network with—perhaps forming a supportive mastermind group to inspire you to keep your marketing campaign fresh, alive, and successful.

Marketing Rule #2:
Have a Distinctive Brand

Your brand is basically composed of a name, logo, color scheme, tagline, and story. What defines your brand is the gut reaction or feeling someone gets when they look at your business through marketing materials, your signage, your website, or the interior of your space. There are lots of books and resources online about creating a distinctive brand, so we will only cover the basics here, but we recommend you thoroughly research the importance of branding.

Just One Social Media Success Story

YoGanesh Yoga opened its doors with one marketing promotion done through Living Social, which netted them a couple hundred students and started the studio off with a bang. However, after a few months, the studio had stopped doing any marketing, and very few new students were coming. Finally, in YoGanesh's third year in business, the owner hired someone for a very reasonable weekly rate to keep her website lively and run some Facebook campaigns. The result: July of her third year in business was her best month ever financially (and July and August are usually the worst months of the year for yoga studios)!

Let's start with your story. Your studio's story will be what you would write in the "about" section of your website. Here is where your mission and vision will be laid out and woven together to tell the story of why your studio exists. In writing this story, hopefully you'll find inspiration for a name, then colors and a logo, and somewhere in between a tagline. Go back to the "Om" Work section of *Chapter 2, What Does Your Dream Studio Look Like?* and play with your vision board in order to have a good starting point for your brand.

If you haven't the faintest idea what your logo should look like and you don't know a great graphic designer, don't worry. Through an amazing online resource, www.99designs.com, a crowd of graphic designers will compete to design your logo based on the information you provide. If you choose one of the designs, that person will get paid. If you don't, you get your money back. Logo design starts at about $250. It's a great way to have ten or even fifty different designs to choose from. In fact, for $325 we received over 150 designs to choose from for this book's cover!

How One Studio Got Its Name

The story of the Bamboomoves branding is a great example of this process. The mission/vision of the studio (before there was a name) was to be a place where all people could find health, happiness, and peace through movement and spiritual community. The studio planned to offer classes in a yoga system that mixed hatha yoga with East Asian internal and external martial arts and dance. There was a major Zen influence, but the goal was something more dynamic and not too martial. Andrew remembered reading about the four saintly plants of East Asia, and immediately bamboo stuck out as a word that he wanted to use. When Andrew googled "bamboo," he read things like: "it grows quickly even in adverse conditions"; "it is strong yet supple" and "long and flexible"; best of all, "its strength came from the fact that its inside was empty." Reading this made bamboo a very powerful image and created a perfect "story" as well as logo inspiration. As Andrew was walking home from work one night after reading about bamboo and reflecting on it for about a week, the name "Bamboomoves" came in a flash and it just felt right. Immediately after, he thought of the tagline: "where your body, mind, and spirit moves." Once Andrew had the name, story, and tagline, he started thinking about colors and the feel he wanted the logo to emanate. It was decided that the logo should look clean, simple, modern, and hip, so it ended up being just the word Bamboomoves and a circle with a piece of lucky bamboo inside it.

Marketing Rule #3: Make an Irresistible Offer and Follow-Up

It all starts with an irresistible offer. The best way to get new students in the door is to offer them something that seems too good to be true. Offers like "30 days of yoga for $30" will really get people excited and make them willing to try a new studio or give yoga a try for the first time. Remember, you are not just competing with the one or two other local yoga studios or gyms in your area for people's time and money; you are competing against *CSI Miami*, *NBC Nightly News*, or reading the morning paper. In other words, you need to convince people to give up some of their free time and give yoga a try. In order to do this, you need an offer that gets people's attention and eliminates *any* financial barriers.

---

30 for $30 Works!

How we know that the offer "30 days of yoga for $30" works? Yoga for Everybody first opened in 2004 with an introductory offer of "first class for $10." This evolved to a second "new student only" offer of "2 weeks of unlimited yoga for $20." In a one-on-one meeting at a three-day training called MindBody University (MBU) in 2009, MBU's founder, Beverley Murphy, recommended increasing the time frame to 30 days. Janis was worried that no one would sign up, and she didn't want to give too much away, but eventually she took a chance and tried "30 days for $49." One year later, at another MBU, Beverley proved to Janis with Yoga for Everybody's numbers that changing the introductory offer to 30 days resulted in a higher conversion and retention rate. Janis then dropped the price to 30 days for $30 at Beverley's recommendation, which led to an increase in the number of people signing up for this irresistible offer. (Read more about Beverley's background on our Acknowledgements page. We will have more nuggets of her wisdom to share in future chapters.)

In the next chapter, we describe and endorse a popular attendance software system called MindBody Online, which we both used for our studios. MindBody Online data from over 20,000 businesses shows that for the average yoga studio, about 50% of the people who try your studio will come back once, but only 25% stay with it long term. Therefore your follow-up offer is just as important as your irresistible offer. The key to your follow-up offer is that it must be a commitment of slightly more time and slightly more money and be time sensitive. If someone signs up for your intro offer of 30 days for $30, and has attended three classes a week for the first two weeks, it seems very likely that person would renew the membership at the end of the month. However, market research shows that after two weeks, most people tend to slump in their exercise-related memberships *unless* they pay for some sort of additional service that re-motivates them.

In order to help new students make a stronger commitment to their own health and well-being, we recommend to have some secondary offers that are sent via automatic email halfway through your students first 30 days of yoga. An example could be: within thirty days of your first class, sign up for a private yoga lesson or a Beginner's Yoga workshop for 50% off! Or the classic: sign up for any class package or membership within thirty days of your first class and receive 20% off. These two simple secondary offers will allow students to make a stronger commitment to their yoga practice and hopefully deepen their appreciation and motivation to practice. The best news is that market research shows it takes approximately 13–28 days for someone to make a new life habit, so if you can hold students' hands through the first two months of their yoga practice, they could become students for life. We will talk more about the best secondary offers and how to grow your yoga community in *Chapter 6, Turning Streams of Income into a Waterfall.*

Marketing Rule #4: Your Brand and Offer Need Multiple Platforms to Sit On

Once you've figured out your brand, irresistible offer, and secondary offers, you need a way to get these messages out to the public, and you need to go at this from various angles. The more times people see your collateral or brand in their life, the more they trust it. Below is a list of various ways you can get your brand and irresistible offer out into the marketplace.

Web Presence: Your Web presence, which includes a website, social media, email marketing, and review sites, is such an important and integral piece of your marketing that we are devoting the entire next chapter to it. In today's era of Google, your website is the foundation of your entire brand. A healthy Web presence can be a total game changer for your business and makes getting new students a breeze.

Flyers/Guerilla Marketing: A well-designed postcard, featuring your irresistible offer and placed into the hand of a potential customer, is phenomenal marketing. In cities, it is easy to spend an hour a day passing out these postcards outside your

> **Market Your Irresistible Offer**
>
> At Bamboomoves in NYC, we would pass out about 3,000–5,000 cards a month on the street. We noticed a direct correlation between the number of new members in a month and the number of cards we passed out on the street. In certain months when we got lazy and passed out fewer cards, we saw a drop in the number of new members. Don't get lazy. This is the sort of practice that many owners do when they first open but then stop. Don't stop.

nearest subway stop. The key to handing out flyers on the street is to look great, smile really bright, and truly attempt to make eye contact with people as they are approaching. Most importantly, don't be offended if they don't want the card. If you continue to emanate positive energy and wish that everyone passing you by has a great day, then you will be able to deliver a ton of postcards. You can also place these postcards at local shops, cafés, doctors' offices, in a card dispenser attached to your building, or on an A-frame sign in front of your building. In smaller towns, you can walk through town and place the cards on people's windshields or doorsteps (though this may be illegal, and could result in a fine). You don't need to spend a lot of money on the postcards; they can be designed and purchased cheaply online from companies like www.99designs.com, www. vistaprint.com, and www.1800postcards.com.

How We Refined Our Guerilla Marketing

When Bamboomoves first opened, Andrew was successfully using guerilla marketing by passing out brochures on the street. The brochures told the Bamboomoves story, and had the schedule, bios of the two main teachers, and an offer for the first class at $5 or a Holistic Health Check-Up for $50. The brochures were text-heavy and costly to print. One and a half years later at MBU, Andrew learned that the only information you really need on your guerilla marketing collateral is your "irresistible offer," which he changed to 30 for $30, a great picture, and your contact information. Making these simple but potent changes dramatically increased the number of new students at Bamboomoves and also saved money, as postcards are cheaper to print than brochures.

Signage: This may sound simplistic, but the bigger the sign, the better, especially the word *YOGA*. Of course your sign should have your logo on it and its colors should be in alignment with your brand. If your zoning allows it (or if no one complains), we recommend you get a sandwich board or A-frame sign with the word *YOGA* that you can place on the sidewalk in front of your studio. Better yet, attach a plastic cardholder to the sign to hold your postcards with the irresistible offer so they are available to all who pass by.

Grand Opening: You will want to put on some major promotions for your grand opening. This is the only time we will ever recommend offering free classes, but it's a good strategy when you're first opening the studio. You want the place packed for that first week or two to create buzz, and the best way to do that is to offer free classes. After that, you'll never do free again! Remember that you still need to have some great secondary offers ready so people can buy class packs or memberships even during the free grand opening.

During this time you will also want to send out a basic press kit, or press release, calling in all the favors you have from local media and friends in the community. We recommend that you begin advertising your studio's opening with postcards and your website at

Moment of Glory

After the hard work of finding a space, hiring teachers, and setting up the support systems, Yoga for Everybody opened its doors on December 26, 2003. The first week's classes were free, with the grand opening taking place on 1/1/2004. One of Janis's most vibrant life memories is of the first Saturday-morning class during that free week, standing outside the doors of her studio, seeing one of her teachers with a room full of people. She had dared to dream, and here it was. She'd imagined something and then created it with guts and determination (and plenty of help!), and now it was right in front of her. Her baby was born.

least three weeks before you open. At this time you may be tempted to do an ad in a local newspaper or magazine, and our official opinion on this is that if you have $400 to drop on advertising, you should use it for Google AdWords or to pay someone to run some social media campaigns (which we will discuss in the next chapter). The *only* reason we would recommend running local ads would be if you wanted to focus on the demographic of fifty-plus and baby boomers, as they are the only demographic that reliably reads local newspapers. If this is your ideal market, then consider running some ads in your local paper(s).

This is also the time to consider Groupon or Living Social coupons—but be sure you limit the number that can be purchased! In the case of an NYC studio, three thousand one-month memberships were sold for $15 each. The studio was actually too full and they only made $0.75 per person per class. Students were not getting the best experience (because of the crowds), and it took months before they completed fulfillment of these one-month unlimited programs. It would have been good for the studio, and the students, to limit the number of memberships that could be sold to five hundred.

Conclusion

Marketing is an ongoing effort and a reality of life in our capitalist society. But we will add that the best marketing is of course the experience that you give every student that passes through your doors. Their experience will come in through all their senses. Is your studio clean and quiet? Is there incense in the air? Did the students feel welcome? It is up to you and your studio staff, teachers, and even other students to create the optimal yoga environment. New students should receive tours of the studio and hopefully individual attention from both staff and teachers. If someone knows their name, they will feel like a part of the community. If they are doing a private session with you or another teacher, help them get the most out of their introductory offer. If they have a fantastic experience, come several times, and then convert to being a member, they will tell other people how fantastic your studio is. Their friends may also ask them why they look so radiant, or seem so calm or happy. And they will be so grateful that your marketing brought them to you.

"Om" Work

1. Gauge your comfort level with marketing and prepare to get started by asking yourself these questions:

    -   How do you feel about advertising and marketing?
    -   Are you prepared to make phone calls to clients and ask people to become customers?
    -   Are you comfortable asking businesses to post your flyers?
    -   Do you know how to create marketing materials such as flyers?
    -   What marketing-related tasks would make your skin crawl?
    -   How can you make marketing fun?

2. Brainstorm your studio's tagline and logo. Get ideas from your vision board and the mission and identity questions you answered in *Chapter 2, What Does Your Dream Studio Look Like?*

CHAPTER FIVE

Web Presence: More Than Just a Website

The Internet is becoming the town square for the global village of tomorrow.

—Bill Gates

A ccording to Merriam-Webster's dictionary, *google* is now a recognized verb. People are so used to turning to the Internet for information that it's likely that people who hear about your studio from an ad, your sign, or a friend are going to run a Google search for your studio from their mobile device, tablet, or computer. These days, your Web presence is much more than just your website. It's your website, mobile site, social media, email marketing, review sites, and online registration and sales capabilities—plus who knows what new Web functions will be introduced in the years to come. It's important to note here that the single most important marketing tool in the world today, Web presence, is essentially free. It can be grown with a consistent effort; business owners (or employees) who spend at least 1–2 hours a day focusing on it will get an enormous bang for their buck. As we said in the last chapter on marketing, a healthy Web presence can be a huge boon to your business, so it's time to dive into the world of the Web!

Your website and Web presence must

1. be easy to find;
2. be geared toward engagement;
3. be easy to navigate;
4. be in line with your identity; and
5. highlight your irresistible offer.

In this chapter we'll explore each of these important characteristics in more detail.

But first, in order to get your website up and running and be able to incorporate all of the items above, you will need two things: Web design/editing software and online business management software. There are many software solutions out there for managing your Web presence and online business, and we suggest you run a Google search to do your own research on this matter. We endorse two particular companies and their products for managing your business. The first, for your website and all Web marketing, is **Live Edit Aurora** (<u>www.liveeditaurora. com/yogaadvisor</u>). The second company, for managing student attendance, online and in-house sales, online registration, and inventory, is **MindBody Online** (<u>www. mindbodyonline.com</u>), or MBO for short. Live Edit and MBO have recently connected their APIs (which is nerd lingo for "their software systems are integrated") so that now your students will never have to leave your website to make a purchase. As we continue to explain the important elements of your website and Web marketing, we will often add that Live Edit or MBO can take care of these elements for you automatically, which is why we recommend them so highly. (If you sign up for MBO through our link, <u>www. mindbodyonline.com/yogaadvisor</u>), you will get your first month free. You can access this link through either Janis or Andrew's websites.)

Now, back to the list of essential characteristics of your Web presence.

1. Easy to Find

Keywords: Set up the right keywords so your website will be easy to find. Live Edit does this automatically, but if you are making your own website with another company, ask them how to input keywords and include words based on your location, your offerings, and specific names of poses and yogic terms like "chakras" and "half-moon pose."

Is Technology Your Nemesis?

Are you confused already? *Keywords* are metatags that live beneath your website and tell Google and other search engines what your site is about. If your brain does matsyandrasana when tech words like this pop up, then do one of the following: a) call your nearest tech-savvy relation, or b) take two down dogs and go to www.getliveedit.com in the morning. Afterwards, go get a massage. You will feel better.

Website Profiles: Make sure your studio has a profile on Google Maps, Bing, Yahoo, Yelp, Facebook, City Search, Jill's List, Trip Advisor, and any other review site you can find. Keep your information current and add pictures and descriptions of your space. People are much more likely to visit the website of a business with positive reviews and pictures. The more you get your students to write reviews on all of these sites, the higher your website will show up in Google, Bing, and Yahoo searches, and therefore the easier it will be to find. Don't be afraid to ask students and friends to write positive reviews. This work can be tedious when you first open up, but then it becomes easy to maintain. Also, the more activity your yoga community has through Facebook, the more your studio will be found on Google.

Google Adwords: One more way you can increase the ease with which people find you on the Web is to run a Google AdWords campaign. These are the little ads that show up above and to the right of a Google search. You can Google "Google AdWords coupon" to find links to get $100 of free Google ads. Google will walk you through the process or you can hire a professional. Basically, you pay each time someone clicks on your ad, and if you set up your website right, then you can track how many people who clicked your Google ad actually signed up for an irresistible offer or anything else.

2. Geared toward Engagement

Equally important to being visible online is to have your Web presence actually engage with users.

Fresh Content: Web engagement starts with having fresh and stimulating content on your website. Any Web software that is difficult or expensive to edit will be the end of you. You or an employee needs to be able to make edits to your website *every day*! This is another reason we recommend Live Edit and MBO: because of their integration, when you edit any information in MBO about teachers, class descriptions, workshop dates, etc., it is automatically updated on your website. Also, Live Edit uses cloud-based drag-and-drop technology so you can edit your site from any device with an Internet connection. We recommend changing the main images or videos on your home page at least monthly, but weekly is better. You want your students to check in with your site each week just like you want them to come to class each week.

Pictures and Video: Pictures speak a thousand words, and videos speak a million! Do not overcrowd your website with text. A student will want to get a feel for your studio and see if they fit in. You should have pictures of your staff, yourself, and a variety of students (preferably with testimonials). Get out of the dark ages! If you don't have pictures and video on your site, you are going to lose potential students. You will notice that major websites are more and more video focused; that's because research shows that Web visitors are losing their patience and focus with words and seeking out images, sound bites, and videos. It's so easy to film a video with your smartphone, and immediately upload it to www. youtube.com or www.vimeo.com, that there is really no excuse not to have video on your website. If you are over thirty-five, you may disagree that this is "easy," in which case you can ask any college-age human interested in yoga and they will likely be happy to help in exchange for classes.

Edits on the Fly

It's 6 a.m., the snow is coming down, and the roads are slippery. You get a call from your 9:15 a.m. teacher; she doesn't feel it's safe to drive. You spring out of bed; within five minutes you've canceled the class in MindBody Online so any pre-registered students are alerted via email about the cancellation. This cancellation is automatically updated to your website as well. You tag a list of students who have taken this morning class within the last six months (also from MBO) and send an email to them announcing the weather-related cancellation. At 6:30 a.m., you relax with a cup of tea.

Email Marketing: Another, more traditional way to engage your students with your Web presence is through email. Most studios have a monthly, biweekly, or weekly newsletter that acts as their main communication platform with students. As people's inboxes are getting more and more inundated with emails, we recommend sending no more than one email a month to your whole student body. Instead, consider editing your website once a week and posting to Facebook every day so that your website and Facebook page become the place where people interact online with your business. Live Edit has a built-in email marketing template that will look identical to your website design—a great way to have consistent branding. There are also plenty of sophisticated email marketing companies like Constant Contact, MailChimp, and i-Contact; most offer a free trial or a free account option, and they are all relatively easy to use. MindBody Online allows you to set up automatic emails to go to students, tailored to the packages they buy, their attendance patterns, and more. Students appreciate a happy birthday email or a reminder when an expiration date on a class card is approaching.

In Defense of Emails

Some yoga centers have had great success sending weekly or biweekly email newsletters to their entire mailing list (which could be 1,000–5,000 or more addresses!). You could send a Monday email with a very specific announcement in the title, such as "Free Healing Circle This Saturday Night". This email will only be opened by people who are curious or interested; the rest of the recipients will delete or ignore it. Your second email, called "This Week at XYZ Studio", can be announcing that week's special events (all of them), as well as any changes in the schedule, who the substitute teachers are, and any additional community news. Students who like to read this every week will look forward to receiving it. At Yoga for Everybody, we found Thursday morning at 7 a.m. to be a great time to send it out, as people are looking for what yoga to take that weekend! Especially if you don't or aren't planning to use Facebook, newsletters are another option for your marketing plan.

Social Media, The Big Whoopie: Currently the most popular way that your Web presence engages with your constituents is through social media. There are hundreds of e-books and lots of free information online about using social media; we recommend you do more research yourself. In this book we will lay out some engagement guidelines for use of Facebook and Twitter. On both platforms, the more your posts get re-tweeted and shared, the more you increase your Web presence and the more "buzz" you get. Posting or re-tweeting something that makes you personally feel emotion, like an inspiring landscape picture or an amazing quote, is a great way to start. Another technique is to ask your constituents questions. For example, ask, "Killing time at the front desk. Tell me: What's the best thing that happened to you this week?" You will be pleasantly surprised when a student posts back, "taking a yoga class at your studio!" On your studio's Facebook page, post regular status updates, and each week post new pictures in which you "tag," or identify, individual students. Twitter is as much about following amazing

Who to Follow on Twitter?

Follow other people or companies on Twitter that are related to your studio's mission and vision. We recommend following yoga teachers and industry leaders and companies that you admire. If your studio is socially conscious, you might also follow some "green" companies or animal-rights organizations. You will want to be following the type of people or companies who are tweeting things you want to re-tweet. It's about being in the conversation and sharing great information with your followers. For example, here are some of the people and organizations Andrew (@AndrewTYoga) currently follows: marketing guru Seth Godin (@ThisIsSethsBlog), a web designer whose work he loves (@ericaheinz), four industry-related companies (@elephantjournal, @Yoga_Journal, @YogaAlliance, and @KripaluCenter), as well as Positive Psychology author @TalBenShahar and super foodie @michaelpollan.

and inspiring people as it is about tweeting, and who you follow says a lot about who you are.

If you're not willing to tweet or re-tweet 5–10 times a day, just stick to Facebook. For those of you who don't even have a Facebook or Twitter account yet, hire someone to help you out—go check the bulletin board at your local café, barter with a college student, do something! Social media is here to stay, so don't miss the boat on this supersonic marketing tool.

3. Easy to Navigate

This point pertains mainly to one's website and one's mobile site. What's a mobile site, you ask? That's a site that is designed specifically for viewing on a mobile device like an Android phone or an iPhone. According to market research, as of October 2012, the number of smartphone users in the United States is currently over one hundred million (mostly using Apple iPhones). That's one hundred million Americans connected to the Internet nearly all day long! You want all your links and site designs to be readable on a mobile device. Make sure you are not running Flash code in your site (that is soooo 2008), because Flash videos and graphics are not viewable on iPhones and iPads. A really cool function of Live Edit is that while you are editing your website, you can see an iPhone example in the right-hand corner of the screen that shows you a mobile version of your design. Other software solutions may also have this function, though typically for an additional fee. If you are using free website software like WordPress, you will have to design an entirely different mobile site or use a plugin.

For both your regular and mobile websites, make sure that students can find what they are looking for quickly and easily. The fewer clicks they have to make, the better. It should be very easy to find the most important information: your schedule, prices, irresistible offer, contact information, and directions. If someone has to click four or five links to get your phone number or see what time classes are today or register for a class, they may lose interest or get frustrated before they get there. Considering that more than 30% of the time people are browsing from a mobile device, one cannot underestimate the importance of economy of clicks.

4. In Line with Your Identity

The colors, branding, and design of your website, social media pages, and email marketing template should all be consistent with your studio's look and feel, marketing materials, and exterior signage. Your mission and vision should be somewhere on your website, and all the pages on the site should have a consistent layout. One common issue when people design their own website is that each page is laid out differently. When you use software like Live Edit, or other template-based Web-design software, you can ensure that each page will have consistent formatting, font sizes, and colors.

5. Highlight Your Irresistible Offer

One final point about your Web presence, is the importance of highlighting your irresistible offer. As we explained in the last chapter, Marketing on a Budget, your irresistible offer is the cornerstone of your marketing campaign, so make it easy to find on your website, social media sites, email marketing, etc. A potential student should be able to sign up for your irresistible offer and pay online without ever having to make a call to your studio.

Your irresistible offer should be so visible on your homepage that it is practically calling out to an observer's eye. This is termed a "call to action." We learned this at MBU and it really works! With one click, the potential student is brought to a page where he or she can enter in payment information and purchase the offer. With Live Edit and MBO, this can all happen on the same Web page, and that student's contact information will instantly be stored in your MindBody Online system, as will the record of their purchase. An automatic email will be sent to them with a receipt and advice on their first class.

Conclusion

This chapter is chock-full of helpful tidbits about building your Web presence, yet it barely scratches the surface. We could have written (and probably will) an entire book about the topic. We hope this brief introduction helps you understand how critical your studio's Web presence is and how powerful it can be as a tool to grow your business. Yogis who aren't tech savvy can tend to shy away from this aspect of marketing because it takes them out of their comfort zone. If that's your case, we beg and plead with you to either bite the bullet and start practicing the yoga of the Internet or hire someone who lives and breathes it. By building a robust Web presence, you will set yourself up for incredible success.

"Om" Work

Run a Google Maps search for yoga studios within a twenty-mile radius of where you want to open up. Check out the Web presence of each studio and notice what you loved, what "call to action" buttons they use, and what turned you off. Then do the same thing for yoga studios in major cities like NYC and L.A., because they have the highest potential to be at the cutting edge of marketing.

Make a video of yourself telling the story of the inspiration behind your studio and your vision for what it will be like. Post the video to YouTube and share it with at least three friends. If you haven't done this before, this assignment may require you to go to www.youtube.com, take a tutorial, and start learning the basics. Imagine looking back at this video on the opening day of your studio.

Go to www.mindbodyonline.com and click their "call to action" button to get a demo of the software. See what they can offer you. We have learned so much about the business of yoga from the good people at MBO, who are gurus in their own right.

CHAPTER SIX

Turning Streams of Income into a Waterfall

Coming together is a beginning.
Keeping together is progress.
Working together is success.

—Henry Ford

So far, we've covered all the bases on how to attract new students. But that's just half the battle. Now you have to retain them. This chapter is about designing your yoga studio offerings to take anyone from yoga newbie to card-carrying *sangha* member. Here we will offer tips and strategies for maximizing your studio's multiple income streams:

1. classes
2. private sessions
3. workshops and retreats
4. teacher training
5. community events

It's important to understand how each one of these offerings helps you achieve your mission and vision and how they affect your business's bottom line. Your various offerings and pricing need to weave together like a tapestry so that students are led on a developmental track from beginners to experienced practitioners. As your classes and community grow, so does your bank account!

1. Classes

In order to attract students in the necessary numbers to build a viable studio, you need to offer classes seven days a week for fifty-two weeks out of the year. Hopefully, you've remembered from *Chapter 1, Is Yoga Studio Ownership Right for Me?*, the importance of designing your schedule so you as the owner have adequate time for self-care, vacations, and personal development. Unlike you, however, your studio should rarely rest. This can be achieved by having trusted employees who can run the show while you're away. In the early days, you might close for major holidays, but once your community has a core group of teachers and students, you will be able to turn holidays into great *sangha*-growing, PR-generating business opportunities. Tempted to close for a week? You'll be giving up revenues while still paying rent, and your students may decide to try other studios to get their yoga class in.

Holiday Yoga Ideas

On Earth Day, have a Yoga off the Mat workshop and free yoga classes in a public park. On Labor Day, perhaps cancel morning classes. Cancel only your evening classes on the Fourth of July. Offer "Will Teach for Food" yoga classes on Thanksgiving to benefit a local food pantry. Christmas Eve and Christmas are great times to reach out to the Jewish community.

Pricing and Payment Options: Keep your class payment options simple. The less math involved, the better. After your irresistible offer, we recommend a single-class drop-in price between $15 and $22, a ten-class package that is 15% cheaper per class than your drop in, and a monthly unlimited-yoga auto-pay option that is no less than $100 a month. You can save one-year-membership offers or other one-time deals for special occasions or slow months like February and December when your finances might need a boost. However, if you offer special deals too often, you lower the average amount paid per class. Some studios offer so many different class packages that students become confused; this can lead to them needing "more time" to decide.

Pricing Should Encourage Retention/Commitment

Contributed by Beverley Murphy, MINDBODY LLC

- Yoga Studios have notoriously low retention (meaning students don't come back) and low average attendance (the average yoga student only comes to class 4 times per month). One of the best ways to improve retention and make more $$ is to create pricing that encourages commitment and more frequent attendance.

- Your students will always purchase the cheapest, lowest commitment option -- which is often a single class or drop in! This may seem great – because they are paying a high price per class but if they don't come back, or they don't come very often, you are losing money in the long run. SO, drop-ins/one time and low class cards/session packages should be expensive

- Memberships/AutoPays and high class card packages should be perceived as "a great deal" (remember, they will actually make you the most $$ over time). What you lose in "price per session" you make up for in retention, commitment, increased attendance and revenue

- You want your students to buy the highest commitment pricing option that makes sense for them

- If there isn't enough of a price difference (savings) between a drop in and bigger packages…they won't buy packages.

- If there isn't enough of a price (savings) difference between 5 session card and a 10 session card... they won't buy the 10 session card.
- Higher volume should be cheaper per class– low volume should be more expensive per class. At Costco, you only get discounts for buying a lot of something.
- Too many pricing options create: Confusion, Indecisiveness, and Reduced sales.
- You should only have around 7 pricing options or less. Studies show that more than 7 options and consumers won't make a decision.

The Importance of Monthly Unlimited-Yoga Auto-Pay: To build community and your bank account, you *must* implement a monthly unlimited yoga auto pay system. Beverley Murphy told us that "according to data collected from thousands of businesses by MBO, this offering is the best way to go from striving to thriving." For the very reasonable price of $100 (or more) per month, students will be able to come to yoga as often as they like. In return for this generous offer, your bank account will grow as these students' credit cards are automatically processed each month. It also helps to smooth out your cash flow. Have a written contract for this option (available through MindBody Online). The monthly unlimited option really makes financial sense for students who would like to come to yoga two times a week or more. As your membership numbers grow, so will your sense of community. Consider offering membership perks like discounts on workshops or clothing.

Designing Your Schedule: How many yoga classes should you offer when you first open? A minimum of fifteen classes a week; 17–20 is ideal. There is no reason to have more than twenty classes a week when you first open as they will not have proper attendance and will lose you money. A schedule of 17–20 classes would include a class every morning (starting between 9 a.m. and 10 a.m.) and every weekday evening. The next important offerings would be a second morning session on Saturday and Sunday, and an afternoon session on Sunday. Then four more evening classes on Monday through Thursday, and finally a Sunday-night class. This is a sample schedule for a new studio offering 18 classes per week:

Smart Class Scheduling

Many studio owners are tempted to offer one class in an early-morning time slot for people to take before work, or one mid-day class for people on their lunch hour. In our experience, getting a following of students when only offering one class in a particular time slot is challenging. Wait until you can offer two, three, or even four classes a week in that time slot.

	Monday	Tuesday	Wednesday	Thursday	Friday	Saturday	Sunday
9:15 AM	All Levels	Level I	All Levels	Level II	All Levels	All Levels	All Levels
10:30 AM- 5:00 PM						11:00 AM Level 1	3:30 PM Yoga Basics
5:45 PM	Level I		Level I-II		All Levels		
6:15 PM		Level II		Yoga Basics			
7:30 PM	All Levels		All Levels				
8:00 PM		Level I		Level II-III			

As your studio gets more popular, and class sizes are consistently averaging fifteen students or more (or if you are in a city or highly populated area), begin to add more classes. Eventually, your studio's schedule may evolve to have up to 35–45 classes a week. It might look like this:

Monday	Tuesday	Wednesday	Thursday	Friday	Saturday	Sunday
8:30 AM All Levels	8:30 AM All Levels	9:30 AM Level II-III	9:30 AM Level I-II	8:30 AM Level I	9:00 AM Level I-II	9:00 AM Level II
10:00 AM Level I	10:00 AM Level II			10:00 AM All Levels	10:30 AM Level I	10:30 AM Level I-II
1:00 PM Gentle Yoga	11:45 AM Yoga Basics	12:00 Noon Yoga Basics	11:30 AM Yoga Basics	12:00 Noon Yoga Basics	12:00 Noon All Levels	12:00 Noon Yoga Basics
	4:00 PM Level IV		4-30 PM Kids Yoga (ages 7-11)		2:00 PM Level 1	2:00 PM Mediation
6:10 PM Level I-II	6:10 PM Level I	6:10 PM Live Music Class All Levels	6:10 PM Level I-II	6:10 PM Level I-II	Workshops	3:30 PM All Levels
7:45 PM All Levels	7:30 PM All Levels	7:45 PM Level I-II	7:30 PM Level I	7:30 PM All Levels		6:00 PM Level I

The above schedule is from Bamboomoves Englewood, a studio that has been in operation for more than three years. The Saturday-morning class will always be your most popular class of the week. It will also be a class that people will bring friends to, so we recommend making it an All-Levels or Beginner class that is taught by your best teacher. Offer Yoga Basics classes once or twice a week on a weekday and a weekend to bring new people into the studio, especially those beginners who need to come in slowly and safely. Bamboomoves offered this class at 12 p.m. to attract the older retired community, but this class can also be effective on a weekday night, drawing in working professionals who are timid about starting off in a Level 1 or All Levels class.

All the yoga classes will be ongoing and people can join at any time. There are no seasonal sessions and no beginning and ending dates. This is true with intro or Yoga Basics classes as well. Ideally, you will have a variety of teachers, so no teacher is on your initial schedule more than 3–4 times a week. It is also wise to have a teacher who teaches Monday at 9:15 also teach Wednesday at 9:15 so people who like her can take her class twice each week. (And the same on Tuesday/Thursday mornings, and Tuesday/Thursday nights, etc.) Do not offer the same type of class back to back or let the same teacher teach back to back. Doing so will reduce the class size, and it will make your life miserable if the teacher has an emergency and you need to find subs for two classes. Trust us on this! If you want to help your teachers make more income for their time, then try to schedule private sessions for them to teach before and after their classes. (Hopefully you have an extra room where those private sessions can be held.)

When you first open, your average amount of revenue per person per class will be lower because of your irresistible offer. Over time, in order to achieve an average of $10 per person per class, offer drop-ins at or above $15 and 10-class pack options at no less than $120. Some studios with low overhead can do well financially with only a class-based stream of income, in which case private sessions and workshops become icing on the cake. How do you know how many classes to start with and grow your bank account? Here is a good formula: Your goal is fifteen people in a class, paying an average of $10 each. That's $150 income per class. Your teachers are going to get approximately $50 a class (we cover what to pay teachers in more detail in the next chapter, *Building and Managing a Great Team of Teachers*), you need to pay yourself $50 a class, and the rest will pay your expenses like rent, utilities, marketing, etc. If your rent is $2,000 a month and utilities and marketing are an additional $1,000, then you need at least fifteen classes a week to cover your expenses, including teacher salaries, and still pay yourself $3,000 a month.

If your rent is $5,000 a month, or you want to invest in a studio manager, how could you raise the additional revenue you need? You would need to add at least five more classes a week that average fifteen students a class, or have a diversified business plan with a robust stream of income from private sessions, workshops, retreats, and teacher training. The good news is that, as you will read shortly, these other offerings will also increase your class sizes, so it's a good bet to have a strategy around them.

You can use the MindBody Online software to pull a report of your average attendance per class and per teacher to see how close you are to your goals. In the above scenario, if you were able to increase average attendance to seventeen students a class, then your yearly income as the owner would go from $36,000 a year to $50,400 a year. And that is without factoring in income from private sessions, workshops, retail, or teacher trainings.

2. Private Sessions

Students who work one-on-one with a skilled yoga teacher or healing-arts practitioner will be more invested in their yoga practice and health. When students get individualized attention they reflect on their lives; they start to put a higher value on self-growth and transformation. As they feel acknowledged, seen, and understood, they will come to more classes and be more interested in workshops. They become a part of the studio's *sangha*. Sometimes when a student who is struggling in her life takes the time to connect with a yoga teacher one-on-one, a beautiful transmission occurs that is at the heart of yoga. Something the yoga teacher or healer says or does can facilitate a dramatic positive shift in the student's life. A private session could be one-on-one yoga, Reiki, or other healing work; you could also rent to or offer sessions with health practitioners who provide complementary services like life coaching, Ayurvedic health coaching, nutrition, acupuncture, massage, or chiropractic.

To complement the "30 days of yoga for $30" irresistible offer, we recommend a second one: a "30-minute Yoga Check-Up for $30." In this one-on-one Yoga Check-Up, students work with a teacher to learn the alignment for basic postures and the names of poses and terms like *asana, pranayama,* and *shavasana.* The teacher learns about the student's limitations or injuries and provides the safe and sacred space for the student to develop the skills and competence to feel ready for and comfortable in group classes. Some students will discover that they want or need extra instruction or help. This is a great way to get students to sign up for regular private yoga sessions. Students can also be encouraged to take a private lesson every month or so to check on their progress as part of their yoga education and development.

What do studios charge for a typical private session and what do teachers get paid? Typically, a one-hour private yoga lesson ranges from $60 to $120 depending on the teacher and location. You will want to do some market research for your area. You can also offer a package such as five sessions for $450, or one private session a month for $75 when paired with a monthly unlimited membership. It is typical to pay the yoga teacher or practitioner 50–70% of the cost of the private session. Or some studios just rent out their private room to the teacher for $20–35 an hour. If you are going to have Yoga Check-Ups as part of your offerings, you can give your teachers an incentive if the student they are working with signs up for any additional packages. An example would be to pay the teacher a higher percentage of 65% instead of 60% if they sign the student up on that day for a package of yoga lessons; or 5% commission if they sign the student up for a monthly membership or sessions with a complementary practitioner.

3. Workshops and Retreats

While private sessions help students go deeper in their yoga practice with one-on-one attention, workshops provide another level of motivation by building community and fostering friendships among your students. There are really two types of workshops that your studio can hold:

Guest Presenter Workshops and Standard Curriculum Workshops.

Guest Presenter Workshops: You can hire an outside teacher to come and lead a workshop based on his or her specialty. Examples may include: restorative yoga, yoga of various styles and traditions, or experiential self-study workshops. The normal split to pay a guest presenter is anywhere from 50/50 to 60/40 presenter/studio. The split could be 70/30 if the presenter is world famous and guaranteed to fill the house with their own marketing power. Generally it is not worthwhile to do too many workshops with outside presenters unless they are teachers who teach in your studio regularly or who are on the level of a Sean Corn, Shiva Rea, or Dharma Mittra. With each workshop you will have to design marketing materials and a campaign that you can essentially never use again. All for 40%! Your popular teachers have the best chance of filling workshops because they can promote themselves every time they teach. You will want to begin marketing workshops at least six weeks in advance; 8–10 weeks is better. Offer early bird pricing so you'll know in advance if a workshop is viable or needs to be canceled.

Standard Curriculum Workshops: Your own unique studio or lineage branded workshops are a good way to maximize your workshop marketing and income, as well as to foster a shared ethos of study. We recommend a series of four workshops so your students will deepen their yoga practice systematically over time: Beginners, Level 2, Level 3, and Level 4. The Beginners workshop runs every month and new students are highly encouraged to take it. It should run two hours maximum and be priced less than $30. The Level 2 workshop is 3–4 hours long, held every two months, and costs no more than $65 dollars. The

Level 3 workshop, held every quarter, could be a six-hour day, on a Saturday or Sunday, for around $150. Finally, the Level 4 workshop could actually be a weekend retreat that happens twice a year; the price could range from $300 to $600 depending on your location. The price points and times are designed to reflect the fact that your target market in each workshop consists of students with progressively more interest and investment in their yoga practice. It's harder to convince total beginners that they should pay $600 or even $65 for a "workshop" when they've never tried one before. You can also offer discount packages that lump all the workshops together or a discount if they sign up for the next workshop on the day they finish the previous workshop. (Please do not allow students to take workshops that they are not yet ready for.)

Designing your workshops in this way will make it easier for people to continually commit to their spiritual growth. Even better, you will have one marketing campaign for all four workshops that lasts all year long. Also, you can hire your local teachers to teach for a standard fee or a smaller percentage like 40% because your system is doing all the marketing. Enthusiastic

Sample Curriculum

Beginners Workshop:Sun Salutes, basic Sanskrit, brief history of yoga, explanation of six main postures with props and modifications, ujjayi breathing.

Level 2 Workshop: Alignment of standing poses and twists, intro to eight limbs and koshas, deeper reflection on yama and niyama, alternate nostril breathing, and kapahalabhati.

Level 3 Workshop: Alignment of back bends and inversions, Ayurveda and nutrition, deep pranayama experience, meditation introduction.

Level 4 Retreat: Yogic diet observed, social silence between sessions, deep pranayama and healing experience, sharing circles, energy anatomy: chakras, nadis, granthis.

83

students who had good experiences will encourage new students to do the workshop and your *sangha* will grow. Sometimes students will want to take the same workshop more than once! You might even allow students to take the same workshop again for a discounted price.

What's the curriculum in the workshops? That is up to you and based on your studio's yoga tradition. In any case, your curriculum should be taught by an experienced yoga teacher and practitioner who is a living example of the benefits of yoga. The best part of a developmental education strategy is that the students who pass through all your workshops will have found something truly worthy of spending their money on and will be begging you for more retreats and a teacher training program.

4. Teacher Training

Because this book is about starting a studio, we will not spend too much time on teacher training. We feel that it is unwise for a studio to offer teacher training in its first year without focusing on building a *sangha* first. Teacher training can be incredibly lucrative and thus tempting for new studio owners to try right away. However, teacher training also requires a lot of work, research, and commitment, and it will cut into your ability to take care of all the other aspects of your business. We recommend considering teaching some weekend-immersion trainings before offering a 200-hour YTT. Another option is to invite a reputable teacher training program or skilled teacher from outside your studio to run a teacher training at your school.

5. Community Events

Community events provide the quintessential experiences that will unite your *sangha*! It's best to schedule these events far in advance so that you can market them and give people plenty of notice. We recommend that you have one free event a month like a *kirtan*, healing circle, or movie night. Every quarter, you should have a staff meeting (we will go into detail about this in *Chapter 7, Building and Managing a Great Team of Teachers*), and you should throw parties two or three times a year. Halloween, holiday seasons, and the anniversary of the studio's opening are great times to host an amazing studio celebration. You can have the celebration be potluck and family-friendly, and make sure to provide great entertainment. Bamboomoves would always have *asana* performances, belly-dancing, open mics, and *kirtans* at their parties, and sometimes funny skits as well.

Show your community of yogis how to have a little wholesome fun and your students' love for you and your studio will grow deeper and deeper. Your community events will also be a powerful way to recruit new students. Consider yearly or even quarterly open houses. Offer 30-to-40-minute sample classes on a Saturday afternoon. Try classes like Meditation, Back Care, Introduction to Yoga, Introduction to Mindfulness, and Vinyasa Yoga. You can think of these events as a way to increase your studio's retention rates, but it is of course more than that. It is your mission, your vision, and it's *fun*!

Responding to Tragedies

Sometimes your sangha will want to respond to a world tragedy by getting together and raising money, awareness, and consciousness. These events are important; they grow your karmic bank account and are likely in high alignment with your vision.

Conclusion

Your studio's offerings can be set up in a developmental way where classes, private sessions, workshops, and community events are all feeding one another. This synergy will increase your class sizes and catapult your profit margins into the stratosphere. Make sure you are on a developmental path yourself, solidifying your place in the *sangha*. Over time, your studio will develop a sense of community that will be palpable to all.

"Om" Work

Reflect on your yogic path. Start by journaling about your first yoga experience; remember how you felt as a beginner. Think of what sorts of skills and knowledge were most helpful to you at that time. What was missing? What would you have liked more of? Start writing down ideas that you can use to design your beginners workshop. Repeat the process for the rest of your yogic path and continue jotting down the various skills, knowledge, and experiences you had that transformed you. Finally, write down the skills, knowledge, and experiences that you still wish to have and choose one to focus on for the next month.

CHAPTER SEVEN

Building and Managing a Great Team of Teachers

The mediocre teacher tells. The good teacher explains. The superior teacher demonstrates. The great teacher inspires.

—William A. Ward

If you've never been a manager before, get ready for the ride of your life. The qualities you need to be a good manager are compassion, principles, and an unwavering commitment to your studio's mission and vision. This sort of strong leadership will inspire your employees to feel part of your team. The teachers are also a lens into your community via their classes, so you want to welcome their feedback and concerns. The focus of this chapter is on how to build a great team of yoga teachers, while avoiding major pitfalls that can ravage your business. In this chapter we will cover:

- Who to hire and how;
- What to pay;
- Establishing a teacher agreement; and
- Managing your teacher *kula*.

1. Who to Hire and How

First, you need to estimate how many teachers you'll be hiring. Then you'll find teachers, interview them and make offers to some of them. Here are some suggestions about hiring teachers.

- How many teachers you need to hire depends on how many classes you and any business partner(s) might be teaching. If you were to hire teachers to cover fifteen classes, for example, you'd probably be hiring about five teachers. If someone teaches more than three classes a week and she gets sick, you'll be scrambling to get subs—or you will be the sub. On the other hand, if you have a teacher who only teaches one class each week, the students who want to take a second class with her will be out of luck. We recommend that each teacher get a minimum of two classes a week in order to build a relationship with students. The only exception is teachers for specialty classes like prenatal or restorative that might only happen once a week.

- Make a list of teachers in your area. If you don't know who they are, find out! Search the Internet, look at who is teaching at other studios or YMCAs, and ask teachers you know who they recommend. Check listings on major registries like the Yoga Alliance (www.yogaalliance.org) and Kripalu Teachers Association (www.kripalu.org/find_a_teacher). As a last resort, place an ad in your local online Craig's List (www.craigslist.org).

- Interview the teachers. Meet with each one for at least one hour. You want to feel comfortable with your teachers, and the impression you make on them will influence how they feel about your studio regardless of whether they work there. Ask open-ended questions like "Why did you get into yoga?" "What was your deepest yoga/healing experience?" and "What is your vision for your career?" Let them know what you are looking for—great teachers who are reliable, stable, and personable team players. Be prepared to talk about what you will pay. If you have a teacher agreement, you might want to give them a copy at this time. Also, find out what class times they are willing to teach. In the "Om" Work section of this chapter you will brainstorm about the qualities you are looking for in a teacher.

Trust Your Intuition

If you get a funny feeling in your gut when you are considering hiring a teacher, pay attention. If the person you are interviewing has concerns about your pay or anything else, dig a little deeper with them. Name it! "Would you be willing to work at this rate and be happy?" Notice also what they don't say, and whether you feel a connection with this person. Leave your "people pleaser" out of the hiring decision.

- Experience their teaching. You can do this before or after the interview. You might feel obligated to hire friends, but this can be a mistake. Don't make any promises to anyone while you are in the planning phase of your studio and be mindful of the "people pleaser" saboteur within. Would you want to take their class? Make sure you *love* their teaching, and also find out first-hand if they are comfortable with feedback. This means you need to give them constructive feedback as a test. After all, they will be joining your team, and you need to be able to talk with them about ways to grow, especially if you notice their class attendance is dwindling. If you've already opened your studio, you can give teachers an "audition" by having them sub a class.

• If you decide you want them to be part of your team, make them an offer. If you haven't already, give them a copy of your teacher agreement.

Teachers Will Find You

If there's no other game in town, or once your business's reputation is established, yoga teachers will be calling on you for an interview. This can actually get to be time consuming! Janis ended up hiring teachers that she didn't make time to interview, because in a pinch they were emergency substitute teachers and the feedback on their teaching was excellent. Andrew experienced the same thing at Bamboomoves and always made it a rule that the teacher in question had to take his class before he would even consider them.

2. What to Pay

How you handle teacher pay can be the difference between your studio's financial success or failure. New studio owners often think that paying teachers per student is a good way to start up and save money. Class sizes can be small (even empty), so giving a teacher $6 a head, for example, *seems* like a great way to save money. However, when your studio is full of students, you will be giving away your salary and your profit! Your teachers will be thriving, while you took all the risks and are barely scraping by.

Depending on your financial situation, we have two different recommendations for how to pay teachers.

• If you are strapped for cash, pay teachers *per head* up to a certain cap. (Note: Do not include students who are using your irresistible offer in your head count.) A fair deal is $3 to $4 per student with a maximum pay of $60. A good rule of thumb is that you *never* want to be paying teachers more than 40% of the income that comes in from a class; the other 60% covers the studio expenses and your salary. When you are strapped for cash, you really need more like 70% of the income to pay expenses and your salary, so don't give this money away. Once you are financially solvent, you can create a base pay and possibly raise the cap.

- Do you have start-up capital that covers your expenses for six months to a year? Are you a master marketer that will fill your classes in the first three months? If so, then pay teachers a fixed amount per class up to twenty students. For teachers with big classes, you can eventually add a per-head bonus around $1–2, with a reasonable cap. With this strategy you will pay more in salaries when you first open but be better off in the long run. Find out what the going flat rate for teachers is at local gyms and other studios in your area, and stick to that amount. It is probably somewhere between $25 and $50 per class.

- Note: Do not raise the flat rate or per-head amount until your studio is so successful that you have hired all the administrative staff you would like, you are taking vacations, and you are paying yourself a decent amount for all the investment you made and the risks you took.

3. Establishing a Teacher Agreement

The first decision is whether your agreement with your teachers will be verbal/informal or written. Here are some of the pros and cons to having a written agreement:

PROS:

- It puts expectations and understandings in writing.

- It shows level of commitment for both the teacher and the studio.

- It puts in writing policies that protect your studio, such as a non-compete clause.

- It describes the teacher's job and makes requests in writing, such as volunteering at open houses.

- An agreement is a great place to have your mission statement. Everyone is on the same page—the mission statement can always be referred to.

CONS:

- Some teachers won't sign it. It's perceived as "not-yogic" (so is running a business!).

- You might be restricting the income potential of some of your teachers.

- It may contradict the nature of your teachers being "independent contractors" (a legal concept described in the next chapter, *Protecting Yourself and Your Business*).

We think a teacher agreement is a good idea, and it's best to have one in place early on. Here's a short list of what goes in a teacher agreement: your mission, pay, policies (see "Managing Your Teacher *Kula*," below), an ethics agreement, and your non-compete clause.

The most controversial piece in the contract is probably the non-compete clause. A non-compete clause benefits the studio, but not necessarily the teacher. A non-compete policy helps to build a strong sense of community in your studio between your teachers and students. Teachers are loyal to the studio, and support both it and each other. They aren't building their own following so much as they are supporting your studio's community to grow. The sense of community will be palpable and a strong magnet for current and new students. It could also weed out some candidates who plan to open a studio near you eventually. Here are some of the components of a non-compete clause.

- Where can they teach? You might allow teachers to teach in gyms and YMCAs, but not at local yoga centers, dance centers, or Pilates centers.

- What's the distance from your studio? The radius clause is part of the non-compete clause. We suggest between five and fifteen miles.

- Grandfather them in. If you hire someone who is already teaching a class within your radius clause, you can "grandfather" her situation in—make it an exception to the rule.

- Make exceptions—in writing: Give your teachers permission to ask for a written exception to the radius clause, on a case-by-case basis. If you have a teacher who wants to offer vinyasa three miles down the road, and she only teaches extra-gentle yoga at your studio, you aren't going to lose any of her students to the other studio.

It's ideal to hire a teacher who is lucky enough to not be financially dependent on the money she earns but is teaching for the love of it. She may have a full-time job, or be raising children, but teaching at your studio is making her day. She doesn't have to do any marketing, rent a space, clean up, or set up—she shows up, does what she loves, gets to soak up the positive vibes, and goes back to her busy life. She will gladly sign your non-compete clause.

Exceptions Made

When a big-box studio opened up down the road from Janis's studio, one of her teachers wanted to teach there. Janis didn't want to lose this teacher (her teaching was excellent and she contributed to the studio in so many ways), so they came to an agreement, and the teacher took on three classes at the other studio. Sometimes you have to break your own policies, and let your teachers spread their wings, hoping they'll later come back to the nest. This same teacher ultimately bought the studio from Janis!

For teachers who are making a living teaching yoga (or trying to), teaching at your studio a few times a week may not be enough. Encourage your teachers to develop niches and programs that they can specialize in as a way to brand themselves and be more marketable to other teaching opportunities outside your radius clause. Also encourage your teachers to offer their programs and workshops as well as private lessons at your studio.

The second most controversial piece of the contract is proprietary information. Students' information is proprietary and cannot be used or shared outside the studio. Teachers should not collect student emails and phone numbers, and should not be emailing students their newsletters. Teachers should not be advertising the other places they work, for example, though of course they will answer questions a student might have. You don't want a student who comes to your studio and takes classes from multiple teachers to start getting email newsletters from all of them, do you? Information should come from one source—your studio.

4. Managing Your Teacher Kula

Each teacher will come to the studio with different strengths and weaknesses *beyond* their yoga skills, such as:

- Do they help build a yoga community? Do they encourage what is best for the students?

- Do they show up on time and end on time? Do they make sure the attendance of late arrivals is noted in the computerized attendance system?

- Do they remember to lock the studio and close all the windows? Do they leave things neat and tidy?

- How often are they sick, on vacation, or away for training?

Here is the reality:

- some teachers will leave you;

- some will drive you nuts; and

- some will bring you great joy and help you grow as a business owner and a human being.

Here are our best tips for making the management of your teachers more joyful and easy:

- have studio policies and procedures in place
- have a substitute-teacher policy
- hold teacher meetings
- know when (and how) to let a teacher go

Studio Policies and Procedures: Put in writing as much as you can. Give a copy to your teachers. Policies include: how early should a teacher arrive before teaching? When do teachers submit their invoices or time sheets? How often are they paid? What is your policy about teachers collecting student information? How should teachers handle emergency situations?

Substitute Teacher Policy: Even though this is part of policies and procedures, it's worth its own paragraph. Have your teachers get their own subs, if possible. It will make your life so much easier! Your job as the owner is to

- give your teachers support in getting subs;

- maintain quality control over the teaching offered by subs; and

- step in during emergency situations.

You can provide both support and quality control by maintaining and providing your teachers with an excellent sub list. Have a printed copy at the studio for them to pick up, and send it to them as an email attachment. Ask them to put it in their cars in case they get stuck in traffic! Your sub list should include names, contact info, and the type of classes a teacher can teach.

Needing a sub at the last minute is one of the toughest parts of owning a yoga studio. It helps if you are willing to be that emergency sub!

Teacher Meetings: Teacher meetings will build trust and communication between your teachers and really generate your *kula*. We recommend you hold regular (1–4 times a year) teacher meetings. Start your meetings with a centering and a shared experience of some sort. Yoga, meditation, even a potluck works for this! Giving all your teachers time for a personal sharing or check-in will move mountains in helping build relationships. You want all your teachers to support each other's workshops and classes and not see each other as competition but part of a shared vision and mission. It's great for you to read letters and testimonials from students. Offer gratitude and acknowledgment to your teachers for the magic they bring into your sacred space.

When to Let a Teacher Go: There are two reasons you would want to let a teacher go—if they break your teacher agreement, or if their class size is too small.

- If they don't support the studio's mission or sabotage the program, you may need to let them go immediately. If they are breaking their teacher agreement by teaching a mile down the road, that would also be a time to let them go. If a teacher consistently doesn't show up, document it and let her know that this is a problem. Be firm; set standards; follow through.

- If a teacher's class size is small and you've done all you can to help the teacher through feedback and marketing, let her know that the class size is too small to sustain itself; if it is not of a certain size on average by a certain date, you will try a new class and teacher (or perhaps drop the class). Be firm about this and refer to your budget and your goal to be a viable and sustainable business. Ask her not to announce to the students that the class is in question or that it is being changed / canceled, until you have decided it is the right time to do so. If the teacher tells the students that a class is under scrutiny, the students will come to you with complaints, and this would be another reason you may want to let the teacher go.

Minimum Class Size

If a class isn't averaging ten people, it isn't covering the cost of the teacher and the "rent." If after several months on the schedule, a class is only pulling in seven people during the busy months of January–March, it may be time to take it off the schedule before the slower summer months. We don't recommend, however, that you take a lot of classes on and off the schedule on a regular or seasonal basis.

When you give feedback or have a difficult conversation with a teacher, it's great to use the "Bun–Veggie Burger–Bun" strategy. That is, begin with some positive statements about the teacher, then the "meat" of the issue, then finish by reinforcing the honest positives while being firm about the "meat."

Conclusion

Remember that as the yoga studio owner, compassionate awareness is an important quality. Manage your teacher *kula* with an open heart. Be ready to listen. Support your teachers through the transitions of their lives, while at the same time honoring what you, as the studio owner, need to put in place to run a sustainable business. You might not be able to solve all the problems of the world just yet, but you can model the behavior you would like to see in your teachers through conscious and clear communication.

"Om" Work

Notice what has drawn you to certain teachers in the past and present. Brainstorm on the kinds of teachers you'd like to have in your studio. Make a checklist of your ideal teacher's qualities. Write everything in the affirmative; instead of saying "Not late," say "Always on time." Your words create your world! After making your checklist, brainstorm ten open-ended (how, why, what) questions to ask in an interview. Now you can hire with confidence.

Optional: Begin drafting your teacher agreement and studio policies and procedures.

CHAPTER EIGHT

Protecting Yourself and Your Business

Common sense often makes good law.

—William Orville Douglas

With owning a business come some risks and responsibilities. Anticipating the worst-case scenario can help prevent it from happening. While there are no guarantees, neither of us have ever been sued. We were each in different stages in our lives when we opened our businesses. Janis had a family, a house, and some money in the bank. She wanted to open a yoga center, but she also wanted to protect her assets. Andrew was younger and had less to lose. No matter where you are in your life, it's important to protect yourself legally. Here are a few examples of what can go wrong:

- A student trips and falls and breaks her hip. The student doesn't have health insurance to cover her injuries. You get sued, and so does the teacher.

- Your business goes belly up and you are personally on the hook for the rent for the next five years.

- A teacher walks away with your mailing list and opens up shop a few miles away.

- Money is routinely taken out of your cash drawer.

- Your studio is broken into and your computer is stolen.

We've divided the ways you can protect yourself into five categories:

1. Maintain adequate insurance
2. Incorporate your business
3. Follow smart business practices
4. Make plans for safety
5. Put things in writing

1. Maintain Adequate Insurance

You'll need to get a few different types of insurance to cover different situations. Some of these are legally required (noted below) and some are just a good idea in general.

Comprehensive General / Professional Liability Insurance: This insurance is legally required. It covers your studio and includes you and any of your employees. It may or may not include teachers working as independent contractors. The rate goes up with the size of your facility, the annual gross receipts, the number of full- and part-time teachers you have, and any additional employees. Your policy will cover your business up to some cap (for example, up to $2,000,000 per occurrence, with a total cap of $4,000,000). Your plan may or may not include sexual abuse liability, and there may be other exclusions. It's important to let your teachers know how your policy protects them and how it doesn't. If you are offering other services, such as massage, you will most likely need additional types of insurance.

Unemployment and Workman's Comp: This is also legally required. If you have employees (if your teachers are paid as employees, or you have an office manager), you will need to pay into unemployment insurance and workman's compensation. The amount paid for workman's comp is based on the nature of your employee's duties, and is paid to your insurance company. You file an annual Policyholder Audit Report that lists your employees, a description of their work, and their gross wages and any overtime. There's also an Employer's Quarterly Federal Tax Return to file with the IRS.

Individual Liability Insurance: Ask each yoga teacher to also have their own professional yoga insurance (and provide you with a copy). If you are paying them as independent contractors, then this is a legal requirement. If they are an employee of yours (not teaching anywhere else), they can be covered under your insurance. Check with your insurance company and labor department to be sure.

Property Insurance: If you have a significant amount of retail inventory, and/or an expensive sound system, you may want to have property insurance to cover theft or damage due to water or fire.

2. Incorporate Your Business

We recommend forming an LLC. By doing so, if your business can't pay the bills, you won't be on the hook to pay out of your personal bank account. (If you form an LLC but you also sign your lease or credit card agreement personally, you *will* be on the hook.) With an LLC, you essentially get the protection of a corporation and the tax benefits of a sole proprietorship or partnership. Here are some of the steps to incorporating; find more detailed instructions by googling "how to create an LLC in the state of [enter your state here]".

- Register your name with the State.

- Work with a lawyer to draft, sign, and file Articles of Organization for [Name of Your Yoga Studio], LLC with the Secretary of State. This document states your company's name and address and designates the "Agent for Service"—you!

- If you have a business partner, it is extremely important to first clearly define and write down your roles and responsibilities. Then work with a lawyer to incorporate this document into an Operating Agreement, which includes the type of company you are forming (LLC for example), who the members are (you and anyone else), when your accounting period ends (such as December 31st), and what happens in cases of dispute or if one partner wants to leave. In an exhibit attached to that agreement, note what your contribution to the company will be. Consult with your accountant on this final piece of the Operating Agreement.

- Prepare and file IRS Form SS-4 to get your federal ID number.

- Prepare and file the appropriate state form to get your state identification numbers.

- Check with your town and state to see if there are any other requirements before you open. For example, in Connecticut there is a $250 annual Business Entity tax.

3. Follow Smart Business Practices

Set up your behind-the-scenes operations to run smoothly. Pick the brains of a few business-savvy friends, and keep them on call as your business grows (and you hit speed bumps along the way!).

Have the phone numbers of a good lawyer and accountant: If you receive a notice from the IRS, you may want to run it by these two. In the best-case scenario you have family, friends, or students you can barter with, because legal and accounting fees can add up. Often you will find one of your students or a student's spouse is a lawyer or accountant. These are great people with whom to trade services for classes.

Put money systems in place: Maintain daily cash reports and get a safe for locking up extra cash. Make regular bank deposits. Accepting credit cards helps reduce the losses!

> **Who We Turned To**
>
> Janis had an excellent background in business and experience in overseeing a low-income housing facility, so she knew how to manage a building and a budget. She turned to Juan Scott, who was then the Regional Director of the Connecticut Small Business Development Center, when she had questions about big decisions (like buying another studio). She also had an excellent lawyer (Tom Walsh), accountant (Stan Weiss), and bookkeeper (Gail Smith). Andrew's uncle Harvey made him write a business plan before he would help finance the studio, and his uncle Bobby was his accountant. It takes a village!

Use an accounting software package: As you run your business, you will need to file and pay taxes and withhold appropriate items from paychecks, like contributions to social security. In this day and age there is no excuse for keeping track of income and expenses with paper and pen. Use computerized accounting software. Some examples include QuickBooks and Peachtree. When you can afford it, hire a bookkeeper and consider using a payroll service like Paychex.com.

Manage alarm systems/keys: Depending where you are located, you might want to have an alarm system. However, if you don't have a lot of valuables in the studio, it's easier on the owner (you!) if you are relaxed about handing out studio keys to the teachers and staff/volunteers—then you don't have to be there all the time! Have everyone sign for keys when they take them and return the keys when they are no longer associated with your center. It's also advisable to have a spare key somewhere near your studio (with the owner of the neighboring juice bar, for example). One caveat: keep your cash in a room/place that very few people have access to.

Refund policies: These should be clear, and in writing, for classes, programs, and retail items. We recommend having an "all class and program sales are final" policy. Exceptions can always be made for extenuating circumstances like injury, illness, and emergency. It's important to have this in writing so students can't demand a refund at a later date.

Upside-Down Robbery

Once when Andrew was alone at Bamboomoves doing some accounting, he decided to go in the classroom to practice headstand for a few minutes to clear his mind. He left the classroom door open so he could see if anyone was coming in. Out of the corner of his upside-down eye, he saw a man run in, grab the laptop off the front desk, and sprint out. He was in the subway before Andrew could even get to the bottom of the stairs. From that point on, laptop locks were used to protect the studio's property.

4. Make Plans for Safety

An ounce of prevention goes a long way. Here are some tips to help prevent accidents and how to handle any that do occur.

Clean, uncluttered space: Make sure floors aren't slippery and all props have their place. Lighting in and around your yoga studio needs to be adequate.

Firm procedures to prevent accidents: Teachers should turn up house lights after *shavasana*, before students get up, and remind students to move carefully and mindfully. Don't leave incense unattended.

Procedures if accidents occur: Teachers know to follow CPR procedures. If there is an accident, they know who (you or your manager) to call and when (as soon as possible); incident reports are filled out by the teachers and any staff who witness an accident. Call your insurance company, and keep in touch with the injured student.

First aid: Teachers should be CPR certified (and provide you with a copy). For around $200 you can have a firefighter come to your studio to teach CPR certification training to all your staff. Have a first aid kit at any location where you are offering classes (such as a beach or park). It will come in handy when a student tries crow pose and ends up with a face plant.

5. Put Things in Writing

We have found that oral agreements invite misunderstandings. You may genuinely remember your agreement differently than the other person. Knowing who is responsible for what among teachers, staff, and volunteers can save time and money. Here are some forms you must have.

Waiver/liability form: To be filled out by new students, this waiver includes a clause about knowing the risks associated with yoga and not holding your business liable. It also asks for emergency contact information. Do some homework to check out the language on the forms used by other yoga centers, YMCAs, gyms, and Pilates studios. Include wording like "I understand that participation in the XYZ class is voluntary . . . I assume the full risk of possible injury inherent in any exercise program . . . I release and hold harmless XYZ, LLC, and any teachers or staff it employs. . . . All sales are final; there are no refunds or credits." There is some debate about whether or not these documents will hold up in a court of law; however, they can't hurt, and we are in favor of conscious communication.

Teacher / employee / volunteer agreements: Student information is confidential and proprietary and teachers, employees, and volunteers are not to take student contact information for their own uses or to divulge any private information. (For more details about what to include in these agreements, refer back to the previous chapter, *Building and Managing a Great Team of Teachers*.)

Independent contractor agreements: If your yoga teachers are independent contractors, create teacher agreements that are compliant with what is allowed between a business and an independent contractor in your state. If you are treating teachers as independent contractors, then you have less legal leeway in telling them how to teach their class and where else they can teach. If the IRS decides that your teachers should have been categorized as employees, there can be financial penalties and even criminal consequences. If your teachers are independent contractors, they will be responsible for paying both income tax and self-employment tax. If they are employees, they will not be able to deduct professional development expenses from their taxes. If you want to play it safe with the IRS, you will pay them as employees. This will raise your teacher expense as you will now be responsible for items like social security contributions, and you will have to spend more time on payroll (or hire someone to do it for you). For a new business owner, the logistics of hiring and paying teachers as independent contractors are easier than the logistics of hiring and paying teachers as employees. Janis didn't have any employees on her staff until her third year of business. Andrew always had all his teachers paid as employees. Accountants, lawyers, and bookkeepers are all independent contractors. General managers and desk staff are not. (See this link for more information on classifying workers as independent contractors or employees: http://www.irs.gov/businesses/small/article/0,,id=99921,00.html/.)

Conclusion

Generally, we are in a "feel good" industry where our students are encouraged to listen to their bodies, to be honest, not steal, and be truthful and compassionate. While this is not typically a litigious group, we do live in a litigious society. Have systems in place to ensure that running your business doesn't keep you up at night. Knowing that your insurance will cover a student's injury and having clearly defined policies and procedures to deal with any student or employee issue will give you peace of mind, and it is a lot more effective than sleeping pills!

"Om" Work

Now that we've talked about all the terrible things that can happen, take fifteen minutes to reflect on the good things in your life and attract more good things to it by writing out a gratitude list. According to a double-blind replicated study at the University of Pennsylvania, keeping a gratitude journal is a proven way to make you happier and less depressed. Write down at least five things, people, events, and so on that you are grateful for. Consider making this a daily practice.

Now make a list of all the good things that can happen as a result of opening your studio. How will the teachers and students benefit? Imagine the ripple effects of your yoga studio, out into the families of your students, into your community, and beyond.

CHAPTER NINE

Will I Make a Profit? How Much? (and When?)

There are three ingredients in the good life: learning, earning, and yearning.

—Christopher Morley

So you've figured it all out. You have your mission and vision, you have your ideal space in mind, your marketing plan is in the works, your curriculum and class schedule is in place, and you know what you need to pay your teachers and how to protect your business. Three questions remain: Will I make a profit? How much? And when? You know how to grow the business on the revenue side, but what are the expenses? This chapter will help you determine your unique situation by diving into two aspects that affect your ability to make a profit:

1. Start-up costs
2. Ongoing expenses

Once you've identified your start-up costs and ongoing expenses, it will be easier to predict if you will make a profit (and when).

1. Start-Up Costs

It's very possible to open a yoga studio with $20,000, and you may be even more successful than a person who spends $100,000. We've seen it done both ways; this chapter will lay out the different expense tracks that potential owners can follow. We also encourage you to include three months of your ongoing expenses in your estimated start-up costs, because when you open a studio, it will take a little while to get your revenues going.

On the Cheap: The least expensive version of opening a yoga studio involves a bit of luck and pavement-pounding in finding a space that is ready to use, in a real estate market that's $15–20/square foot. You'd still need to bring in equipment and supplies, and set up your attendance, marketing, and accounting systems, but you'll save a ton on construction. If you have talented and generous friends and family (or if you also have skills, strength, and energy), then you may be able to save on designing the website, creating graphics and flyers, and doing some of the heavy lifting and construction. Under optimal conditions, you could spend as little as $20,000. You will put down a security deposit and first month's rent, perhaps some utility deposits, and prepay your insurance.

Money to Burn: The more money you are able to spend in the beginning, the nicer your space can be and the bigger your marketing campaign can be. You could even hire staff and take time away from your studio for self-care. If money is no object, you may want to purchase new furniture, technology, and equipment. Depending on how much construction your studio needs, you could be looking at total start-up costs of $100,000 or more. Quick note: if you've got money to burn, then instead of splurging on designer chairs for your lobby, do extra marketing.

Here's an example of the difference between the least and most expensive versions of the equipment you need: while a new studio could get by with one computer, or a computer from home, one desktop, one laptop, and one tablet would be ideal (one for the sign-in desk, one for the office, and one that you can take with you). Most likely, your start-up expenses will be somewhere in the middle.

Here is a chart of three sample start-up cost scenarios. In the end, your studio may be a combination of possibilities from all three scenarios.

- Scenario #1: Minimize your spending and studio ready to be used

- Scenario #2: Moderate spending strategy and some building renovations

- Scenario #3: Making your studio the best it can be—in a space that needs a lot of renovation

START-UP EXPENSES	Scenario 1	Scenario 2	Scenario 3	Your Scenario
CONSTRUCTION				
Signage	$500	$1,000	$2,000	
Major construction (architects, permits, walls, doors, plumbing, electric, etc.)	$1,000	$5,000	$50,000	
Heating and cooling system	home or existing	$2,000	$18,000	
New bathroom	use existing	$2,500	$7,000	
New shower	none	none	$2,000	

START-UP EXPENSES	Scenario 1	Scenario 2	Scenario 3	Your Scenario
Paint entire space	$500	$2,000	$4,000	
Add wall or ceiling fans	use existing	$500	$2,000	
New studio floor	use existing	$4,000	$10,000	
Lobby flooring	use existing	$700	$1,500	
Security system (free to install)	$0	$0	$0	
New thermostat	use existing	$200	$250	

FURNISHINGS and DECOR

Lobby furniture	from home	$1,000	$2,500	
Music system and speakers	from home	$650	$4,000	
Coat hooks, shoe racks	$100	$150	$300	
Water filter or water cooler	$30	$300	$500	
Garbage cans (2–4)	from home	$50	$100	
Decorations	from home	$1,000	$2,000	
Window blinds or drapes	use existing	$1,000	$4,000	

LEGAL

Lawyer	use friend / self	$2,000	$4,000	
LLC publishing fees	$500	$1,000	$1,500	

MARKETING

Website design and graphic design	do it yourself	$2,500	$7,000	
MindBody Online software	$70	$70	$120	
MBO key tags	go without	$750	$750	

START-UP EXPENSES	Scenario 1	Scenario 2	Scenario 3	Your Scenario
Flyers, brochures, stationery, biz cards	$500	$1,000	$2,000	
Print advertising for six weeks	none	none	$600	
Google AdWords/ SEO	$500	$1,000	$3,500	
YOGA EQUIPMENT				
Yoga props	$500	$1,200	$2,500	
OFFICE AND COMPUTER				
Office computer(s) or tablet(s)	from home	$1,200	$4,500	
Printer(s)	from home	$200	$500	
Credit card swiper	$50	$75	$100	
Scanner(s) and thermal printer	none	$500	$800	
Basic/electronic cash drawer	none	$50	$200	
External (back-up) hard drives	from home	$100	$200	
Desks and chairs for office	from home	$200	$1,200	
Desk and chair for sign-in room	from home	$300	$1,000	
Cabinet for office supplies	from home	$150	$600	
Telephone(s)	from home	$65	$250	
RETAIL				
Inventory	none	$1,000	$5,000	
Bottled water to sell	$50	$100	$125	
OTHER				
Insurance deposit	$1,000	$1,000	$1,000	

115

START-UP EXPENSES	Scenario 1	Scenario 2	Scenario 3	Your Scenario
Security deposit + 1st month's rent	$4,000	$6,000	$10,000	
Bank deposits to open accounts	$1,000	$1,000	$1,000	
Cleaning products	$50	$100	$150	
Cleaning equipment	from home	$200	$400	
Office supplies	$100	$250	$300	
Keys to building	$20	$40	$100	
Mat wipes	none	$200	$200	
TOTAL START-UP EXPENSES	$10,470	$44,300	$159,745	
ADD 3 MONTHS OF ONGOING EXPENSES (SEE NEXT SECTION)				
TOTAL CAPITAL REQUIRED TO OPEN A YOGA STUDIO				

By reading over the types of expenses you might encounter, you can begin to see the level of investment necessary. There may be some categories of expenses that you hadn't even thought of until this time. As you read over these start-up strategies, take a wide-angle view, without focusing too much on the details, to get a picture of what is involved. By picking which scenario fits your budget, you'll be able to see the sort of studio your unique financial situation will support.

2. Ongoing Expenses

There are two ways to look at ongoing expenses. One is actual cash flow—money in and money out. This is what small-business owners often focus on and what we recommend. The second point of view is an accounting perspective, which looks at your numbers for revenues, expenses, liabilities, assets, equity, and profit. The difference between cash-flow figures and accounting expenses can be small or large, depending on how much you spend on items that cost cash but aren't fully deductible on IRS form Schedule C in one year—such as installing a new floor or carrying inventory. If this stuff makes your head spin, don't fret; talk to an accountant or business coach.

Did We Get Everything?

There may be expenses you thought of that are not on this list. Perhaps you want to take a class to learn QuickBooks before you open, or hire a company to run a focus group to test-market different studio names. (Janis did both of these!) Or perhaps you'd like to buy a $450 Ganesha statue for your lobby? When Andrew was managing Tao Yoga Center in NYC, they budgeted extra money for free food and giveaways during the first month when they had open houses every weekend. Remember, the little things add up.

For the purposes of this chapter and this book, we will be talking about a cash-flow approach when we use the term "ongoing expenses," so this is not an accounting perspective. As mentioned in the beginning of the start-up expenses section, we advocate including at least your first three months of ongoing expenses in the amount of cash you need on hand to carry you through the entire start-up process.

You must create a budget spreadsheet—and you will need this if you are going to take out any loans. In this spreadsheet, you will be projecting monthly revenues.

Rather than estimating based on how many packages you will sell, use an estimate based on the average revenue per student per class. If you are offering two workshops a month at $30 per person and projected attendance is fifteen students, then your estimate for workshops for the month is $900. The different sources of revenues were explored in *Chapter 6, Turning Streams of Income into a Waterfall.*

Sample Budget Spreadsheet

REVENUE	# of Times a Month	Average Attendance	Average $ Per Student Per Class	Total Revenue
Classes	15/wk x 4.2 = 63	15	$10	$9,450
Workshops	2	12	$35	$840
Privates	10/wk x 4.2= 42	1	$25	$1,050
Merchandise				$400
Total				$11,740

Assumptions for the revenue estimates above:

- Fifteen classes/week, fifteen students per class, $10 average revenue per student, 4.2 weeks in a month (15 x 15 x 10 x 4.2 = $9,450)

- Workshops bring in $840 per month, by having two workshops for $35 with an average attendance of twelve students.

- Private yoga sessions: ten per week with rental revenues of $25 per session (times 4.2 weeks/ month) (10 x 4.2 x 25 = $1,050)

- Merchandise—Buy $200 inventory wholesale, sell for $400 retail

The expense section of your budget spreadsheet will include a mix of fixed expenses and variable costs. You'll have fixed expenses, like rent and insurance, and some costs that vary, like total teacher salaries and your electric bill. Below is a list of likely ongoing expense items and sample costs. The second column is for you to fill in your own estimates. You must include your salary as an expense. Remember, paying yourself is not optional; it's a requirement!

OPERATING EXPENSES	Example	Your Scenario
FIXED EXPENSES		
Rent	$3,000	
Insurance	$175	
Utilities	$300	
Telephone	$100	
MindBody Online software	$70	
Live Edit Online software	$49	
VARIABLE EXPENSES		
Office help	$650	
Teacher pay ($45/class)	$2,835	
Workshop teacher pay 60%	$504	
Your salary	$2,500	
Advertising	$300	
Supplies	$200	
Credit card fees (3% of CC sales)	$340	
Repairs	$100	
Retail	$200	
Miscellaneous	$100	
TOTAL OPERATING EXPENSES	$11,423	

Under the above scenario, your revenues were $11,740 and your expenses were $11,423. You made a profit of $317, and also paid yourself $2,500 in salary. (Note that you would have paid yourself additional if you taught some of the classes and especially if you teach privates!) Your profit (and part of your salary) could be used to hire a part-time office manager (beyond the $650 spent on office help) or a part-time bookkeeper, or for your own professional development (such as workshops at the Kripalu Center for Yoga and Health). Please remember that if you do collect a salary, you will need to pay taxes on that income each April.

Will I Make A Profit? (And When?)

When your expenses and revenues match, that's your projected break-even point. Anything above that is profit. Getting expert advice from a business consultant at SCORE (www.score.org) is a great way to put together a cash-flow analysis for your business from start-up through the first five or ten years. Your revenues will ramp up over time, and there is usually some seasonality to factor in as well. As the bottom line starts to reflect a positive number, you are earning income above what you pay yourself. It's very exciting to put together a cash flow analysis on paper that predicts how you will make money and when.

One rule of thumb that can be helpful is to realize that you need a certain number of students in your classes to pay the bills. The more students in each class, the more revenues you are making (without expenses going up). If you have five students in each class, you are probably only bringing in enough revenue to pay your rent and overhead. If you have ten students in each class, you are probably also paying your teachers out of your revenues and not your pocket. This is often the break-even point for a yoga center (but without the owner taking any salary). Once you reach fifteen students in your yoga classes across the board all year round, you are likely able to pay yourself. If your numbers go higher than that, yahoo! You are in the money. Of course, these numbers vary with your particular situation, such as your rent, how many classes you have, how much you pay teachers, etc. That's why you need to make projections.

When you will make a profit depends on your numbers! You can be profitable in year one or it can take several years. You might spend more in the early years, but those expenses could cause you to be more profitable in a shorter period of time. For example, you might buy a competitor's business. You'll have a huge expense that year, but as a result you'll have many more students. Another example is to spend extra money on marketing when you first open. This may require you to spend more than you are normally comfortable with, but it will pay dividends down the road. Remember, marketing works.

Words from Someone Who Should Know

The cofounder of the famed Omega Institute, Stephan Rechtschaffen, offers a workshop on how to start a holistic learning center like the Omega Institute. Janis attended this workshop before opening her studio. She was delighted to hear Stephan repeat over and over again something along the lines of, "It is difficult to make money when you open a holistic learning center, because each program is a one-time event and you have to do marketing for each one. But those yoga studios are making money hand over fist. Once you convince someone to become your client, you receive a steady stream of revenues, potentially for years." Think of it: if you spend $100 in Google AdWords and get one student, and he comes for one year and buys a membership for $108/month, you've generated over $1,200 of revenues from that $100 investment.

Buy Another Yoga Center!

When Yoga for Everybody bought Marleen's Yoga Center in 2005, the business lost money due to the investment, but the studio's average class size doubled while increasing the number of classes as well. This investment was a no-brainer. Sometimes buying a local competitor is a way to get to your break-even point faster while you are expanding your business. In this case, the two owners were friends so the merger was very amicable. Marleen and her staff continued to teach, which led to a high retention rate for her students.

Besides looking at your financial numbers, you'll also want to track some key indicators over time. Fortunately, MindBody Online makes generating statistics easy. We recommend paying attention to trends like: number of visits per month (how many bodies come through the door and take a class or workshop), average number of students per class, and average visits per student. Hopefully, these numbers increase each year. One of the best key indicators is your retention rate; how many new students are you converting to ongoing clients? Which teachers have the most students coming back to their classes regularly? What percentage of students are still coming to your studio six months after completing their introductory offer? Knowing the answers to these questions each month will make you an empowered business owner who can make sound evidenced-based decisions about class times and teachers.

MindBody University

If you attend the three-day workshop offered by MBO called MindBody University, you will learn about all of the ways you can track your business in MBO, and more. You'll also have individual meetings with their faculty to help you make sense out of your unique situation. Andrew and Janis each attended

---

MBU three times before they ever met, and realized while writing this book that they were at the same workshops! These conferences are a great place to meet and swap ideas with other business owners.

Conclusion

If you can't make your yoga studio profitable on paper, DON'T OPEN! Once you open your doors, you'll be referring back to your projections to see how your studio is actually performing. For extra inspiration, you may want to put up a big chart in your office and graph your progress!

"Om" Work

1. Draw up a list of financial resources you have or can draw on to open and run your yoga business. Include your bank account and also estimates of any money that friends/family/colleagues might be willing to pitch in or loan you. See what your grand total is.

2. Look at the risks and rewards of opening your own yoga center. What are you risking? What might you gain? Imagine the worst case and the best. Write it down and sit with it.

3. Find 1–3 yoga studio owners that you can talk to and ask them about their experience in opening a yoga studio. Did they go in with a budget plan and how did their business perform relative to that plan? If you don't want to talk to studio owners near you, contact the owners of studios that inspire you from around the world. People love to tell their story!

CHAPTER TEN

Parting Words of Wisdom

You'll miss 100% of the shots you don't take.

—Wayne Gretzky

Andrew's Top 5

1. **Get *Sattvic*:** I remember once asking Professor Edwin Bryant at a lecture he was giving on the *Bhagavad Gita*, "how does one know what their dharma (purpose) is?" and his answer has always stuck with me. He said: "First get *sattvic*, clear away the clutter in your life, and then simply ask that inner voice, that deep inner knowing that is always there." We tend to want to make changes or decisions in our life when we are not happy or content, but this is a mistake. We must get *sattvic* first. Before you dive into studio ownership, make sure to take time to get away from the normal grind of your life and do whatever you need to do to feel connected to the universe (*sattvic*). Whether it's spending a few days at the beach, going on a silent retreat, or having a weekend to yourself at home, do whatever you need to do to recharge your battery before you make a decision.

2. **Have a Hobby:** Have goals for your own personal growth and health that are not dependent on the

yoga studio. Find a teacher you will study with or a topic you wish to learn more deeply and never let your "business" be an excuse to stop your own self-cultivation. Having an engaging hobby or practice where you are learning something outside of your work life can really help stimulate your creativity and act as a bright spot and salvation when the business is going through challenging times.

3. **Let Go of the Fruits of Your Actions:** It's cliché, but I can't emphasize Krishna's main message from the *Bhagavad Gita* enough. Remember that everything is perfect. Everything happens in its own time and that everything will be OK, no matter what happens. Boom or bust, a business cannot hurt your soul, that part of you which is connected to the divine and is perfect all by itself. It's worth repeating Sri Krishna's quote from Chapter 1 (though with a slightly different translation): "It is better to fail at your own dharma than to succeed at the dharma of someone else."

4. **Don't Jump into a Lease:** Make sure you figure out your vision, mission, identity, logo/brand, website, and marketing plan BEFORE you sign a lease! So many studio owners try to do everything all at the same time. You need to give each element of your business its proper time and attention. Doing construction and dealing with a lease is overwhelming enough, and you want to actually stay yogic while you are getting this business off the ground.

5. **Take the Next Step:** By compiling all your responses to the "Om" Work assignments in this book, you will have essentially crafted a first draft of your dream studio's business plan and hopefully be able to make

an informed decision about whether or not studio ownership is right for you. The next step is to refine your plan with the help of a mentor, coach, consultant, or other experienced business person. Your plan will need a realistic timeline, and considerable research to polish up your budget. The more people you bounce your plan off of, the better. You will learn something from everyone and you will learn from the process as well.

Janis's Top 5

1. **Take Responsibility:** With great success comes great responsibility. Students often come to yoga wanting something different in their lives. It is a privilege and a responsibility to create a sacred space where human beings feel safe enough to begin to peel back the layers of protection they have built up over the years, the layers that now hold them back from an authentic life. By practicing yoga on the mat, people are able to open their hearts off the mat.

2. **Be an Oak and a Willow:** Winston Churchill said, "You have enemies? Good. That means you've stood up for something, sometime in your life." You can't please everyone all the time. By the same token, be open to feedback. You will grow as a person from this business of yoga. You could not ask for a more conscious, loving, supportive group of human beings to hang out with than yoga teachers and students. In the end, you need to be strong, but don't forget to bend when the wind blows.

3. **Get Help:** In *Lord of the Rings: The Return of the King*, Sam says to Frodo, "I could help a bit, I could carry it,

share the load . . ." Invite people to help you! Hire staff sooner than you think you can. Shoot for a full-time manager, or two part-time ones.

4. **Get a Life Coach:** M. Scott Peck said, "Life is difficult. This is the great truth, one of the greatest truths . . . because once we see this truth, we transcend it." Consider working with a life coach to help you transcend the difficulties; with his or her support, you will keep the vision of your thriving studio alive. You will move toward that reality by identifying and setting goals, and then taking steps. How long should you work with a life coach? Forever! There's always a bigger game if you want to keep playing!

5. **Network:** Make friends with other business owners. Having compatriots in your field will help you get through the lows and revel in the highs. Form a mastermind group, where you meet in person or virtually and serve as each other's board of advisors. The group can be all studio owners and managers, or people from a range of industries. When Andrew suggested to Janis that they write this book, it was Janis's mastermind group (of non-yoga entrepreneurs) that challenged her to do it, and held her accountable to make it happen.

6. Oh, wait, there's one more: **Have fun!**

ABOUT THE AUTHORS

Andrew Tanner, BA NYU, E-RYT 500, has been successfully running yoga businesses since 2003. Currently, he serves as the director of the Kripalu Schools of Yoga and Ayurveda, one of the largest yoga teacher training programs in the country, and the Kripalu Professional Association, a yoga teacher membership organization with over 2,300 members. Andrew has helped launch more than eight successful yoga studios, including four with Bamboomoves (which he co-founded), four with Dahn Yoga, and YoGanesh Yoga in New York City. Andrew feels blessed to be serving the yoga community through helping yoga teachers and potential studio owners attain "right livelihood" and make a proper living doing what they love. You can find him at www.andrewtanner.com.

Janis Bowersox, MBA Yale, RYT 200, and Co-Active Coach, combines her business background and management experience with her love of yoga. In 2004, she opened Yoga for Everybody, a Kripalu-affiliated, independently owned and operated yoga studio in Fairfield, CT. She grew the business for six years and then successfully sold it for a profit. Having lived and breathed the challenges and joys of running a yoga center, she is uniquely qualified to mentor studio owners and their managers. She offers life-coaching services to yoga studio owners and their students. You can find her at www.janisbowersox.com.